A Natural History of GIRAFFES

A Natural History of GIRAFFES

pictures by Ugo Mochi
text by Dorcas MacClintock

•

Charles Scribner's Sons, New York

To
T. Donald Carter
who knew and loved the animals of Africa

Contents

Preface

Giraffes in general and Ugo Mochi's giraffes in particular have been the inspiration for this book. Ugo Mochi creates each cut-out, or graphic sculpture, from a single sheet of heavy black paper, even to the delicate tracery of a thorn tree. A pencil sketch is laid over the black paper. Using a small lithographer's knife and a glass-topped working surface, the artist, with agile fingers and infinite skill and patience, cuts out each animal. As a sculptor, Mochi concentrates on form, rather than color or pattern. His animals in outline combine design, action, and three-dimensional form. Spontaneity is captured, giving his animals life and movement. Seldom are the animals cut in profile; more often they appear at an angle, in three-quarter view, or even head on. Perspective is attained without color or shading.

Born in Florence, Italy, in 1889, Ugo Mochi began to cut animals in paper at an early age. Later, when his singing career took him to Berlin, Germany, he met the animal sculptor August Gaul, at work on a wax model of an elephant in the zoo. This chance meeting led to two years of study with the master sculptor. Subsequently Mochi turned to the art of outline as his life work and has received acclaim the world over.

My introduction to the art of animals in outline came during the years of collaboration between Ugo Mochi and the late T. Donald Carter, Assistant Curator of Mammals at the American Museum of Natural History, on their book *Hoofed Mammals of the World*. Each time the artist came to the museum with a newly completed plate, staff and students would gather to admire his work. Of all the cut-outs the giraffes were my favorites.

In the preparation of this book about giraffes, I am especially indebted to Dr. and Mrs. T. Eric Reynolds of Piedmont, California, with whom I traveled to Africa in 1970; to Hobart M. Van Deusen, American Museum of Natural History, in whose office I worked as a student during several summers; to the late William P. Harris, Jr., of Grosse Pointe Park, Michigan, who wrote at length of East Africa as he knew it and who suggested that I correspond with Dr. Anne Innis Dagg. I have been fortunate in having available the library facilities of Yale University, particularly its Kline Science Library. I also wish to thank the following for providing information about giraffes: Jean Hayes, A. J. Deane, and Frank Minot, Jr., naturalists in Kenya; Dr. B. Elizabeth Horner, Professor of Biological Sciences, Smith College; Dr. Margaret Altmann, University of Colorado; Hugh B. House, Curator of Mammals at the New York Zoological Park; and Dr. Friderun Ankel, Yale University. Joseph A. Davis, Scientific Assistant to the Director, New York Zoological Park, kindly read the proofs and made helpful suggestions. Special thanks go to Edna Mochi, wife of the artist, and to my husband, Copeland MacClintock, for their encouragement and helpful criticism.

DORCAS MacCLINTOCK

A Natural History of GIRAFFES

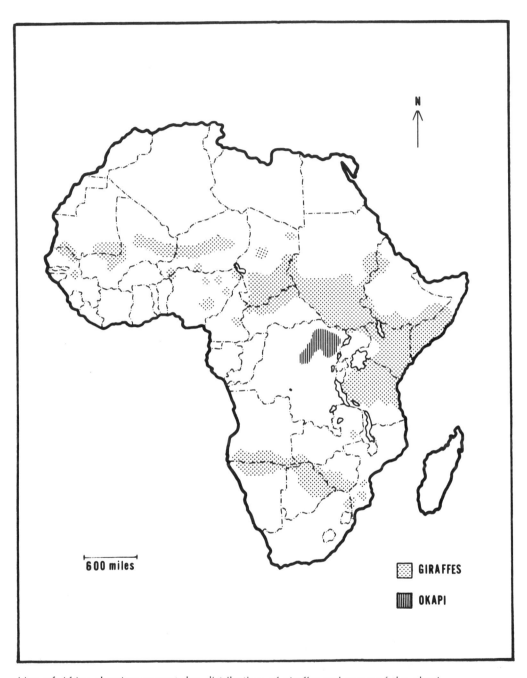

Map of Africa showing present-day distribution of giraffes and range of the okapi

1 Giraffes Today

As I leaned out of the Land Rover's hatch, gazing at the first wild giraffes I had ever seen I thought of a description from a favorite book, Isak Dinesen's *Shadows on the Grass:*

"Praise be to thee, Lord, for Sister Giraffe, the which is an ambler, full of grace, exceedingly demure and absent-minded, and carries her small head high above the grass, with long lashes to her veiled eyes, and which is so much a lady that one refrains from thinking of her legs, but remembers her as floating over the plain in long garbs, draperies of morning mist or mirage."

In the tall, green grassland near the Albert Nile in Uganda the three Baringo giraffes did seem to float over the plain. There was something feminine about them, although all three were large bull giraffes. One of the giraffes browsed on a small bush. The second giraffe looked down with dark eyes that were veiled with long lashes. The third giraffe turned, full of grace, and ambled away with two piapiac birds clinging to his neck.

3

Giraffes range over much of Africa south of the Sahara Desert, preferring dry, open wooded areas or tree-dotted plains. They browse on trees and bushes and often cross large grassland areas to reach another belt of trees.

Giraffe habitat includes various kinds of country: the grasslands and the **nyika** thornbush of East Africa; the **miombo,** an immense belt of savanna (grassland with scattered trees) that stretches across Africa's mid-continent; and the **bushveld,** the belt of dry thornbush that stretches across Angola, South West Africa, Botswana, Rhodesia, and South Africa. Their distribution is affected by man and his spreading populations, his agriculture, his herding of cattle, goats, and sheep, his fencing of land, his poaching activities, and his killing for sport or control of disease.

Classification (or taxonomy) indicates natural relationships among living things. What is known about an animal's anatomy and physiology and whatever traces an animal has left in the fossil record are the taxonomist's tools. Living mammals have been classified into eighteen orders. One of these is the order Artiodactyla, the even-toed hoofed mammals, to which giraffes belong.

All **artiodactyls** have the third and fourth digits, or toes, elongated. The two terminal phalanges (bones of the digits) are encased in a cloven hoof. Broad-crowned cheek teeth with ridged grinding surfaces are also an artiodactyl characteristic.

Some artiodactyls are cud-chewers; others, such as pigs, peccaries, hippopotamus, camels and llamas, and tiny chevrotain are not. The cud-chewers make up a subgroup called the Pecora. They have no upper incisor teeth, just a hard gum pad. Deer, giraffes and okapi, pronghorn, antelopes, buffaloes, cattle, and sheep are all pecorans.

There are nine families of living artiodactyls. Giraffes

and okapi are the two living members of the family Giraf-
fidae. All giraffes have the scientific name *Giraffa camelopardalis.* The genus name *Giraffa* probably comes from an
Arabic word, "zurāfah" or "zarāfah," which has several
meanings: "one who walks swiftly," "creature of grace,"
"lovely one," "tallest of all mammals"—all appropriate
enough for the giraffe. The species name, *camelopardalis,*
refers to two animals, camel and leopard, once believed to
be the giraffe's ancestors. The okapi, found only in the
equatorial rain forests of Zaïre (the Congo), is known as
Okapia johnstoni.

Much of what is known about giraffes today—their
behavior, their locomotion, their spot patterns—is the
result of the work of a Canadian zoologist, Anne Innis Dagg.
As a graduate student, she observed giraffes on a cattle and
citrus farm in the eastern Transvaal of South Africa for nearly
a year. From film footage obtained during her field study,
she later investigated the role of the giraffe's long neck in
locomotion and analyzed the giraffe's peculiar gaits. She
continued her giraffe research in museum collections,
where she found marked differences between the skulls of
males and females. During a year in Australia, she studied
spot patterns in a zoo herd of giraffes of known parentage.
Other scientists have also carried out detailed observations of giraffes in the wild and in zoos. J. B. Foster, a
Canadian, has worked with giraffes in Kenya's Nairobi
National Park. Dieter Backhaus of Germany has trailed
giraffes in Garamba National Park in Zaïre and studied their
behavior in the Frankfurt Zoo.
Countless additional hours of patient giraffe-watching
are needed to learn the secrets of individual giraffes' lives
and to piece together an understanding of their social behavior and their relationships with other animals.

2 In the Fossil Record

The history of the early evolution of the mammals, the class of vertebrates, or animals with backbones, to which both men and giraffes belong, is complicated and not very clear. From many stocks of mammal-like reptiles were descended many kinds of reptile-like mammals. Some kinds survived, others did not. Mammals slowly came into being in fits and starts of evolutionary activity. About 180 million years ago, in the late Triassic, the mammal-like reptiles —called therapsids—reached the point of being reptile-like mammals. The fossil record of these rather small creatures is poor, but some 70 million years ago, at the end of Mesozoic time, their numbers increased. Mammals in many different forms began to occupy the ecological niches left vacant by the fast-disappearing dinosaurs.

Sharing a common ancestry with the deer, the giraffes branched off from their cousins during the Miocene epoch, some twenty million years ago. The first true giraffes occur

6

in the Miocene in Central Asia. *Palaeotragus* is one of the earliest giraffids. Medium-sized, with neck and limbs only slightly elongated, it is presumed to have looked very much like the okapi; and, like the okapi, its two short, pointed, bony horns were developed only on males. The early giraffids lived during the Miocene and into the Pliocene, approximately ten million years ago. They ranged over Eurasia. Most were woodland browsers. *Samotherium* was larger than *Palaeotragus* and, to judge from its teeth, a grazer. *Giraffokeryx* sported four long horns.

The okapi is grouped with the palaeotragine giraffids. Because it has remained much the same since prehistoric times, the okapi is sometimes referred to as a "living fossil." Dense forest habitat and elusive behavior may be reasons for the okapi's survival. At Olduvai Gorge, the Pleistocene fossil locality in Tanzania, East Africa, where for years the late Dr. L. S. B. Leakey and his wife Mary directed excavations, the palaeotragine *Okapia stillei* has been found.

Giraffes prospered during the Pliocene. Two fossil giraffids of this time resembled the living giraffe. Both were large, with long necks and limbs. They roamed over eastern Eurasia twelve million years ago. *Giraffa*, the genus of the living giraffe, occurred in the Pliocene and Pleistocene of Asia. Not until the Pleistocene, one to two million years ago, did it reach Africa. Close relatives of the living giraffe, *Giraffa gracilis*, more light in build, and *Giraffa jumae*, a more massive giraffe, have been found in Olduvai Gorge beds.

The sivatheres, a third giraffid subfamily, were the gigantic giraffids of the Pliocene and Pleistocene of Asia. Heavy limbs supported their oxlike bodies. Their skulls were very large and broad, bore variously developed skin-covered horns, and contained large sinus cavities. Overspecialization may have been the sivatheres' downfall.

Sivatherium ranged over what is now India a million years ago. Two short horns sprouted over its eyes, and two large, palmate horns branched from the back of its skull. A small bronze figure of a *Sivatherium*-like animal adorns a chariot-rein ring made by an ancient Sumerian more than three thousand years ago. This archaeological find suggests that sivatheres still lived when this early civilization flourished in the Middle East.

Another sivathere, *Bramatherium*, bore two huge upright horns on top of its skull, and another short pair projected laterally from the back of its skull. *Hydaspitherium* had a single skin-covered bony "boss" on top of its skull, formed by fusion of two large horns. *Helladotherium* was an enormous hornless giraffid with camel-like proportions. Remains of another sivathere, *Libytherium olduvaiensis*, have been found at Olduvai.

In 1970 limb bones of a late Pliocene giraffid were uncovered in Russia, indicating that warm climates then prevailed far to the north. Toward the end of the Pliocene climates became increasingly cold, and many of the giraffids vanished from the earth.

3 Spot Patterns

Giraffes have their buff-colored hides covered with spots of darker brown. These spots vary in shape from smooth polygons to jagged blotches. Body spots are usually large, while spots on head and legs are small. No two giraffe patterns are identical. The first major classification of giraffes was presented by the British naturalist Richard Lydekker in 1904. He divided the true spotted giraffes into ten subspecies on the basis of range, coat color, spot pattern, and horns. The reticulated giraffe was considered to be a separate species. However, variations in spot pattern and horn shapes make these difficult characteristics to use in the designation of giraffe subspecies.

Geographical trends can be found in giraffe spotting and coloration. There are five types of markings: spotted, reticulated, jagged, leafy, and blotched. Spot color ranges from pale yellowish-brown to nearly black, on ground colors of white, tawny, or yellowish. The reticulated giraffe,

9

SPOTTED

RETICULATED

with its dark chestnut color and network of narrow white lines, is found in northeast Africa. Just west of its range is the Baringo giraffe's territory. This giraffe's lighter-colored patches are separated by a network of wide buff-colored lines. Farther to the west are found the true spotted giraffes. From the Equator south, in Kenya and Tanzania, giraffes generally have dark spots, jagged or even leafy in outline, on yellowish or tawny body color. In South Africa giraffes have large, well-defined blotches. Nine giraffe subspecies are currently recognized.

Giraffe Subspecies

Northern	Ranges	Markings
Nubian giraffe *G. c. camelopardalis*	Eastern Sudan, fairly common; also found in northeast Zaïre	Large, quadrangular chestnut spots on buff-white background
Kordofan giraffe *G. c. antiquorum*	Western Sudan; scarce	Much like the Nubian giraffe except for the very small size of spots on upper legs
Nigerian giraffe *G. c. peralta*	Nigeria, Niger Republic, Senegal, Chad, Cameroon; except in Chad, rare	Very large; spots paler and more numerous than the Nubian giraffe
Reticulated giraffe *G. c. reticulata*	Somalia, Ethiopia, north and east Kenya; common	Large, liver-chestnut, polygonal spots separated by network of narrow white lines or reticulations
Baringo giraffe *G. c. rothschildi*	Uganda (over 1000 estimated); also some in southern Sudan, west and south Kenya	Very large size; pattern similar to the reticulated giraffe's except that white lines are wider and neck pattern is blotched rather than reticulate

Southern	Ranges	Markings
Masai giraffe *G. c. tippelskirchi*	Kenya, Tanzania; common	Jagged or leafy spot pattern on yellowish background; lower legs spotted
Thornicroft's giraffe *G. c. thornicrofti*	Zambia; 200 to 250 individuals estimated	Leafy pattern; median horn often well developed; spots on lower legs
Angolan giraffe *G. c. angolensis*	Angola; fairly numerous	Large body spots; spotting on lower legs
Transvaal giraffe *G. c. giraffa*	South Africa, South West Africa, Botswana, Rhodesia, Mozambique; numerous	Spot pattern starlike or blotched; legs spotted to hoofs

In the natural world there are exceptions to every rule, and so it is with giraffe spot-pattern trends. Northern giraffes (the first five subspecies listed) generally have no spotting on their lower legs, but the reticulated giraffe is often spotted below the knee and hock. Southern giraffes have darker colored legs that are spotted, often to their hoofs. The median horn tends to be less conspicuous in male giraffes of the southern subspecies, but again there are always exceptions.

Because all living giraffes belong to a single species, *Giraffa camelopardalis*, they interbreed. In zoos this has led to a confusion of spot patterns, for often the parent giraffes have come from different parts of Africa. Even in Africa giraffes in the same area exhibit varied spot patterns. In a herd of four giraffes observed in northern Kenya, only one giraffe had the narrow network pattern and liver-colored, geometrically shaped spots of the reticulated giraffe that one expects to see here. A second giraffe had the brown, oak-leaf spot pattern and tawny interspaces of

JAGGED

LEAFY

BLOTCHED

the Masai giraffe, usually found in the southern half of Kenya. The other two giraffes were intermediates: their large spots similar to the reticulated giraffe's but lighter in color and notched in outline; their background color tawny rather than white.

Reticulated giraffes also interbreed with Baringo giraffes, their neighbors to the west. Giraffes have been seen, where the two ranges overlap, with characteristics of both subspecies.

Anne Innis Dagg's study of the eighteen giraffes bred from three original giraffes in the Taronga Park Zoo, Sydney, Australia, supplies evidence that giraffes do inherit the color, number, position, and shape of their spots. Perhaps someday a thorough spot-analysis study of giraffes will aid in unraveling the tangle of giraffe subspecies. Number of spots, total area of spots, and shape of spots would have to be considered. The Masai giraffe's most distinctive feature is its very large number of irregularly shaped spots; the handsome reticulated giraffe's spots cover a large body area; the Baringo giraffe's spots cover much less area, especially on its neck.

There are extreme variations in giraffe color. A Masai giraffe bull, so dark he appears almost black, has been seen repeatedly in the Serengeti. Reports and photographs of white giraffes come from parks in Uganda, Zaïre, Zambia, and Tanzania. Most of the white giraffes are not true albinos. Cream-colored, they have dark eyes and often faintly visible blotches. A large white giraffe, photographed in Kenya's Masai Mara Game Reserve in 1971, is white even to his mane and tail tassel. This bull, when last sighted, was the tallest giraffe in a herd of twenty-six.

There are many theories as to why giraffes and other animals have spots. For each theory some giraffes can be

found that "fit" and others that do not. Some naturalists have argued that among acacia trees the bold pattern of the giraffe's hide becomes a "cloak of invisibility." At a distance their spotted bodies are lost in the rippling shadow pattern of moving leaves. Their long necks disappear among the trees' branches, and their long legs resemble the trees' trunks.

Disruptive patterns (spots and stripes) are found in predator as well as prey species. Like the giraffe's blotches, the leopard's spots disrupt, or break up, its body outline.

This causes the animal to blend with its background, at least in certain circumstances, and makes the animal harder to see. When a leopard lies on a branch its spots do seem to match the sun dappling of its riverine-forest habitat, but when a leopard ventures out on the plains its color is hardly concealing. In tawny grass it is the hunting lioness whose hide blends perfectly with the background.

Sometimes giraffes are very conspicuous in their environment. At other times, for all their towering height, giraffes are hard to see. In the shimmering heat and light of midday giraffes at a distance "lose" their spots. Colors of spots and interspaces blend to a typical bushland hue. Watching a single giraffe in the bush, one may suddenly become aware that there are five, six, or more giraffes close by.

If protective coloration is to be really effective the animal must stand rigidly still. This the giraffe does not do. Often its head projects inquisitively above or around a tree's leafy top. It flicks its ears back and forth and whisks its tail noisily.

Spot pattern and color have been correlated with position of the sun. Near the Equator, where light and shade are more distinct, live the giraffes whose spots are dark-colored. Farther south, where the sun is less harsh, giraffes have less distinct spot patterns. The exception to this theory is the Transvaal giraffe, a southern form whose dark patches are well defined.

Carl G. Schillings, the German explorer-naturalist who traveled to Africa in the 1890s, had still another idea. He thought giraffes "mingled" with their environment by mimicry. Giraffe form, he thought, was more important than spots or color. He took photographs to show how a giraffe's body outline resembles the shape of a nearby thorn tree.

Giraffes have little need for camouflage. Their chief enemy, the lion, hunts mostly by scent. Safety for giraffes lies in their ability to see great distances.

Dr. Heini Hediger, late director of the Zurich Zoo in Switzerland, suggested that a giraffe's blotches may be used

in the "optical marking" of territory. Territory is an individual animal's, or in the case of the giraffe, the herd's living
area. Giraffes share their geographical range and their
savanna-thornbush habitats with many other animals. Simply by being in an area the spot-patterned giraffes mark their
territory. Only elephants and black rhinos are more successful than giraffes in driving other animals out of their imme-
diate area or away from their place at a **water hole.** But
giraffes are not territorial in the usual sense. Herds and individuals move about, and there is no fixed area to be defended
against other giraffes.

4 Giraffes in Form

Head

The giraffe's skull is highly specialized. Relatively large by ruminant standards, it has overcome the problem of its own bony weight by the development of air sinuses. These extensive sinuses, which occupy much of the upper part of the giraffe's skull, make the skull, for its size, relatively light. The sinuses, formed as nasal, frontal, parietal, and supra-occipital bones of the skull grow apart, are filled with thin lamellae, or leaves, of bone. Probably the sinuses occupy "dead spaces," which have resulted from disproportionate skull growth in the course of giraffe evolution. Sinus formation occurs in other mammals; generally the larger the skull, the greater are the areas invaded by air.

The two-foot-long skull of a giraffe weighs anywhere from five to twenty-four pounds. This astonishing range of skull weights was determined by Anne Innis Dagg from studies of fifty-five giraffe skulls in several museums. She

22

found that skulls of male giraffes are considerably heavier than those of females—from two to three times as heavy. Male giraffe skulls averaged twenty-two pounds, those of females only seven and a half pounds.

A male giraffe's horns have a spongy bone texture unlike the female's horns. Halfway down their cylindrical lengths the horns of male giraffes average six inches in circumference, twice the average circumference of the female's spikelike horns.

The male's fondness for indulging in sparring matches accounts for the sexual differences in giraffe skulls. These bouts, called **head-slamming** (or necking or head-hitting) are so commonly staged that two or three contests may go on at the same time within a herd. The giving and receiving of head-slams stimulates deposition of bone, which increases the skull weight. A male giraffe's skull is massive. Bony bumps, or **exostoses,** develop over the skull. The horns, up to nine inches long, enlarge with use; unlike the female's hair-tufted horns, the male's are topped by bare skin caps. The amount of bone deposition depends upon the age of a male giraffe. On an old-timer the bumps sometimes appear as distinct "horns."

Occipital, or mizzen, "horns" are really exostoses sometimes developed on the back of the skull. Possibly they provide additional area for attachment of neck muscles and protect the first and second neck vertebrae. Other exostoses protect eyes and blood vessels.

The giraffe's short, unbranched, skin-covered horns are unlike those of any other mammal. In fact they are the distinguishing feature of the giraffe family. These paired horns are permanent, not shed annually as are the antlers of male deer. Nor do they resemble the true horns of the bovids (antelopes, buffaloes, cattle, sheep, and goats), which have horny sheaths fitting over hollow bone cores.

The development of giraffe horns is also unique. Antlers of deer and horns of the bovids grow out from the skull's frontal bones. Giraffe horns have their beginning as **ossicones,** or knobs of cartilage. In the newborn giraffe calf the ossicones overlie the front parts of the skull's paired parietal bones, their position indicated by tassels of dark hair. Ossification, the replacement of cartilage by bone, starts at the tips of the horns and spreads downward. Pads of cartilage at the bases allow for continuing growth of the horns. At four and a half years the horns of a male giraffe are fused to its skull; it may take seven years or more before horn fusion occurs in the female. By then the giraffe's horns have grown forward on the skull to overlap the suture between the frontal and parietal bones. Even after fusion to the skull the horns of a male giraffe continue to increase in length and thickness by addition of bone.

Development of the median horn appears to be sexlinked. Present in all giraffes to some degree, it is probably formed from an ossicone. In male giraffes the median horn often is very prominent. Its function may be protection of the nasal region of the skull.

The skull of a male giraffe, with its bony reinforcement, is well adapted to the animal's curious mode of fighting. When the powerful muscles of the neck swing the giraffe's head in an arc to slam against another giraffe's body, its backward-slanting horns are very effective weapons.

Teeth

The six lower incisor teeth that bite against the hard gum pad of the giraffe's upper jaw are shaped like spatulas. This suggests their function is combing leaves from branches.

The canine teeth, one on each side of the lower jaw, are also peculiarly shaped. A deep groove makes the canine appear two-lobed. Sometimes a giraffe canine tooth is tri-lobed.

A long diastema, or gap, extends between front teeth and cheek teeth (premolars and molars) on each side of the lower jaw. Like all browsers, giraffes have low-crowned grinding teeth. Their wrinkled, or rugose, appearance dis-tinguishes giraffid grinders from the smooth-enameled teeth of all other browsers.

Giraffes have thirty-two teeth. The dental formula of giraffids, fossil as well as living, is:

$$I \, \frac{0}{3} \qquad C \, \frac{0}{1} \qquad P \, \frac{3}{3} \qquad M \, \frac{3}{3}$$

Neck

In mammals the cervical, or neck, vertebrae almost always number seven. This is a mammalian characteristic that holds as true for the whale whose neck is functionally absent as for the giraffe whose head is balanced on top of a flexible, columnar neck, five feet or more in length.

The neck vertebrae of the giraffe are quite different in appearance from those of any other mammal. The first two cervical vertebrae in all mammals are called the "atlas" and the "axis." The atlas, shaped like a butterfly, has two sur-faces that are in frictional contact with the occipital con-dyles, which are rounded knobs at the back of the skull. This forms a joint that makes possible the up and down movements of the head. In the giraffe the occipital condyles

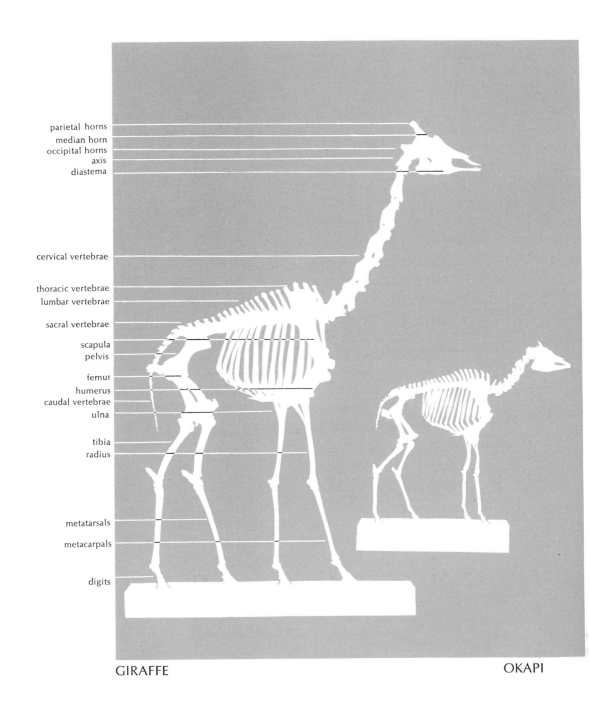

parietal horns
median horn
occipital horns
axis
diastema

cervical vertebrae

thoracic vertebrae
lumbar vertebrae

sacral vertebrae

scapula
pelvis

femur
humerus
caudal vertebrae
ulna

tibia
radius

metatarsals

metacarpals

digits

GIRAFFE

OKAPI

are so well developed that its head can be extended upward as a nearly vertical extension of its neck, an advantage when a tempting green branch is just overhead. The axis has a conspicuous central protuberance, the odontoid process. This fits neatly into the base of the atlas ring and forms an articulation so that the head can be turned from left to right.

The remaining five cervical vertebrae are specialized. They are large, elongate, and tubelike, with low, rounded neural spines. Narrowest and longest (up to eleven inches) are the third and fourth vertebrae; the rest are shorter and wider. Increased length provides more surface area for muscle attachment. Each cervical vertebra is rounded anteriorly (that is, toward the giraffe's head) and fits into the concave posterior of the preceding vertebra. Layers of ligaments hold the vertebrae in place. Vertebrae that form these ball-and-socket kinds of articulation are called "opisthocoelous." This refers to the fact that the cavity (coele) is behind (opisthos), or on the posterior end of the vertebra. Opisthocoelous neck vertebrae, found in hoofed mammals generally, as well as in dinosaurs, provide for flexibility.

Just as its skeleton, like a scaffolding, determines body form, the giraffe's muscles give the contours which make the animal so beautiful in outline. There are muscular as well as skeletal modifications in the giraffe's long neck. Along many of the neck muscles, muscle and tendon alternate. This provides for a combination of force and pliancy; the small stretches of muscle give maximum control with minimum energy waste. The retractor muscle, which has its origin on the front of the sternum, or breastbone, and its attachment on the small, horseshoe-shaped hyoid bone at the root of the tongue, functions to draw back the tongue. In the giraffe the retractor muscle originates on the sternum as a nine-inch, slender, fleshy muscle. It changes into a six-inch-long tendon, which divides, then becomes fleshy again where it inserts on the thyroid cartilage (the movable neck cartilage that is man's "Adam's apple"). This long muscle then continues on to the hyoid bone as a flat sheet of muscle. Other neck muscles, like the paired muscles that extend from skull to sternum, used when the giraffe bends its head down close to its chest, are each a single stretch of muscle.

For support of its head atop its columnar neck the giraffe relies on an enormously developed neck ligament, the **ligamentum nuchae.** Its tough, yellow, elastic tissue has its origin far in back of the neck. Starting on the lumbar (lower back) vertebrae, the ligament passes forward, acquiring additions all along the giraffe's spinal column. The two closely bound halves of the ligament extend up the neck, overlying the low neural spines of the cervical vertebrae. It continues over the first vertebra, the atlas, leaving the atlas free for head-turning movements. Then it attaches on the occipital crest at the back of the skull.

Down the length of the giraffe's neck, from back of head to behind its withers, runs a stiff, brushlike mane that is the color of its spots.

Body

The giraffe's back slopes from shoulders to rump. Slope relieves some of the heavy vertical load of the neck. This part of the giraffe's spinal column is made up of fourteen thoracic, five lumbar, and four or five fused sacral vertebrae.

Each thoracic vertebra—except for the first, which looks like a cervical vertebra—has a long dorsal spine. These spines form the "hump" on the giraffe's upper back and provide additional surface for the attachment of the large muscles and the ligamentum nuchae that support neck and

head. The vertebral spines and connecting ligaments form a web of "struts" and "ties" that gives strength and lightness to the giraffe's back.

Ribs articulate with the thoracic vertebrae. The anterior seven pairs attach to the giraffe's strongly curved sternum; six pairs of ribs fuse with a cartilaginous support to form a basket for the internal organs; the last rib pair "floats"— that is, lacks cartilaginous support.

The first of the fused sacral vertebrae articulates with the ilium, one of the three bones that form the pelvis.

Legs

Much of the giraffe's stature comes from its long legs. The nearly vertical position of the scapulae, or shoulder blades, makes the giraffe's forelegs appear slightly longer than its hindlegs. Size and shape of the scapula—the longest and narrowest of any mammal's—provide a large area for muscle attachment. The absence of a clavicle, or collarbone, is an adaptation for running. In all ungulates (hoofed mammals) the limbs move only in one plane, fore and aft. There is no need for the bony brace for the shoulders, formed by paired clavicles connecting scapulae to sternum, that is found in mammals adapted for life as burrowers, climbers, or fliers.

Almost equaling the scapula in length is the humerus, the bone of the upper foreleg. Radius and a much-reduced ulna, bones of the lower foreleg, articulate with the humerus. The radius extends downward to the carpal bones of the "knee." What appears to be the giraffe's "knee" corresponds in fact with man's wrist. Below the "knee" two of the metacarpals (III and IV), two of the five bones that form man's hand, are fused as a single cannon bone. These two metacarpals are elongated to approximately the same length as the radius. Metacarpals I, II, and V were gradually lost in the course of giraffe evolution.

The giraffe's forelimbs have no bony attachment to the rest of its skeleton. The hindlimbs do. The pelvis, formed by three bones—ilium, ischium, and pubis—articulates with the backbone. The head of the femur, the upper hindleg bone, fits into a socket, the acetabulum, in the pelvis. The other end of the femur is much enlarged and articulates with the tibia, the bone of the lower leg. The fibula, like the ulna of the foreleg, is much reduced in ungulates. This joint, the giraffe's true knee, is sometimes referred to as the stifle. It is equipped with a patella, or kneecap. Tarsal bones, somewhat fused in the giraffe, correspond with the carpals of the forelegs; they form the ankle, or hock. One of the tarsals, the astragalus, provides the main articulation between leg and foot and is specially modified in the artiodactyls, the even-toed ungulates. Curved and pulley-shaped above and below, the astragalus gives the hindleg great freedom of motion in running and bounding. Below the hock, metatarsals III and IV form a single long bone. Sometimes metatarsal II persists in the giraffe as a small "splint" bone.

Movement is always the result of contraction of muscles, which are grouped in opposing, or antagonistic, sets. A foreleg is raised by contraction, or shortening, of one set of muscles; it is returned to the ground not by relaxation of these same muscles but by contraction of another, antagonistic muscle set on the other side of the foreleg. In the living animal the balanced tension that exists between all the opposing muscle sets in the body is called tonus. Never are the muscles entirely relaxed.

The giraffe's limb musculature also shows modifications. Most of the giraffe's weight, perhaps three-fifths, is taken on its forelegs. Its shoulder blade is slung upon two large muscles, one from scapula to chest, the other from scapula to lower part of neck. Elastic cartilages at the end of the scapula, between muscles and foreleg bones, give spring to the forelimbs, on which the giraffe's body balance depends.

Muscles bunched in the upper forelimbs and upper hindlimbs control movements of the lower legs by means of long tendons. With this stiltlike set-up a giraffe can, with contraction of muscle in its upper foreleg, cause its hoof to move in a wide arc. Its leg then swings much as a pendulum, and the giraffe is not encumbered by a muscle-heavy lower leg when it moves.

Hoofs

The third and fourth digits (or toes) of each of the giraffe's large feet are encased in two broad, weight-supporting hoofs. In some artiodactyls the second and fifth toes—or only one—are carried above and behind. These "false hoofs" are missing in the giraffe.

Loss of toes is generally an adaptation to open habitats. Both artiodactyls and perissodactyls (odd-toed hoofed mammals, such as zebras and rhinos) have undergone loss of some digits. Standing on their toenails, they are fast runners over hard, dry ground.

The hoof print of a full-grown bull giraffe measures as much as twelve inches long and is nine inches across, a good area for support of the giraffe's one-ton weight.

Tail

A giraffe's tail is a handsome object. Spot-patterned hide covers the sixteen to twenty caudal vertebrae that make up its length. Above the hocks the tail is tipped by a heavy tassel of coarse, wavy black hairs. Giraffes use their tails in communication, as well as for switching flies.

5 Function

Digestion

Giraffes are **ruminants** (from the Latin word *ruminare*, to chew over again). Between periods of **browsing,** while standing, walking, or lying down, giraffes chew their cud—at the rate of about one chew per second. Sometimes an entire herd stands about ruminating for hours. Browsed food, swallowed whole, is later regurgitated to be thoroughly chewed.

Ruminants have four-part stomachs. The first part, the **rumen,** is a spacious paunch where food is stored and partly fermented. During the process of fermentation the cellulose of the food is broken down by the bacteria and by the cellulytic (cellulose-dissolving) enzymes produced in the stomach by ciliate protozoans (microscopic one-celled animals fringed with "hairs," or cilia). Fermentation produces fatty acids, which pass through the walls of the rumen and into the blood capillaries, and it produces

34

gases—methane and carbon dioxide—which the giraffe gets rid of by belching. Not only do giraffes belch, they also drool. Their alkaline saliva buffers the stomach acidity that results from fermentation, so giraffes never suffer from acid indigestion.

From the rumen food passes into the **reticulum**. This second part of the giraffe's stomach is lined with many small pits. Here cuds, or boluses, which are small balls of food, are formed. When the muscles of the stomach contract, a bolus is forced up the long muscular esophagus; its upward passage is quite visible to an onlooker. The giraffe rechews the cud, on one side or the other, with a rotatory movement of its lower jaw. It takes about forty-four chews to reduce a bolus to pulp. Then, mixed with saliva, the food mass is swallowed. Several seconds later another bolus is regurgitated.

The rechewed food mass passes into the **omasum,** a part of the stomach lined with many folds, and then into the **abomasum,** where it is mixed with gastric juices and chemically modified. From the abomasum the food mass, now in dissolved form, enters the intestines, which are from 260 to 280 feet long. In the small intestine the food undergoes further breakdown and is absorbed through the intestinal walls into the bloodstream. The residue passes into the large intestine, where water is absorbed. Giraffe feces are extruded as acorn-shaped pellets, each about an inch and a half long.

Circulation

A fully grown giraffe, its head sixteen to eighteen feet above the ground, represents a natural experiment in the adaptation of circulation to the stress of gravity. At levels below the heart, gravity tends to increase pressure in the arteries; at levels above the heart, it decreases pressure. Somehow a giraffe's blood pressure is regulated so that the animal does not black out when it lowers its head between bent or splayed forelegs to drink at a water hole. Nor does a giraffe experience giddiness when it flings up its head in alarm.

Two South African physicians, Robert H. Goetz and O. Budtz-Olsen, were the first to investigate the giraffe's unusual circulatory system. In 1954 they set up a field laboratory in the Transvaal. For the anatomical part of their study a pit was dug, eight feet in length and three feet in width and depth, to hold the head, neck, and heart of an adult giraffe preserved for dissection. Unfortunately a gazelle tumbled into the pit, and its flailing hoofs tore the plastic lining. The scientists had to procure new plastic lining and more formalin for preservative before proceeding with their investigation.

Dissection showed the heart to be large, long, and tapering in shape. A tiny curved bone is buried in the muscle of the heart's base. In proportion to the body weight of the giraffe, its twenty-five-pound heart is considerably heavier than the hearts of most large mammals; but, like all mammal hearts, it is completely divided into right and left chambers. Contraction (or systole) spreads, wavelike, over the heart muscle, first affecting the thin-walled atria (receiving chambers), then the thick-walled ventricles (pumping chambers). With each contraction, deoxygenated blood, returning from the giraffe's body, flows through the right atrium into the right ventricle. The inch-thick muscle wall of the right ventricle contracts to force the blood into the pulmonary artery that goes to the lungs. Returning from the lungs as oxygenated blood, the blood passes into the heart's left atrium, then to the left ventricle, where contraction of the three-inch muscle wall forces it into the arteries that supply the giraffe's head and body.

In giraffes and other hoofed mammals, the carotid artery, which carries blood to the head, does not divide into internal and external carotid arteries, as in many other mammals, but extends with few major branches for six feet between heart and head.

Blood pressure is caused by contraction of the heart's ventricles. Blood pressure is sustained by the pressure exerted on the blood by the walls of the arteries and by peripheral resistance to the passage of blood through the small blood vessels and capillaries of the giraffe's body. Systolic blood pressure is measured in millimeters of mercury (mm. Hg—Hg is the chemical symbol for mercury) at the peak of ventricular contraction (ventricular systole), when pressure in the arteries is greatest. Diastolic blood pressure is registered at the lowest ebb of pressure, when the ventricles are relaxed. The difference between these two readings—for instance, 150/115 mm. Hg in man—indicates the capacity of the circulatory system to sustain pressure.

Because of the height to which blood must be raised in the carotid arteries in order to reach the brain, the giraffe was suspected of having high blood pressure. In anticipation Dr. Goetz's team, which by this time included six other medical doctors, had a special instrument that measured up to 600 mm. Hg.

Techniques of immobilizing animals were then little known. The doctors, with some difficulty, succeeded in shooting a female giraffe with a curare-filled bullet. The animal was blindfolded, hobbled, and a scaffold-like pen was built around her before the antidote for curare was injected. A local anesthetic was used to insert an eight-foot catheter (a tubelike device) into the giraffe's neck artery. This bit of surgery was necessary because thickness of hide made it impossible to determine giraffe blood pressure by palpation, or feeling. Blood pressure in the carotid artery at the base of the brain, some ten feet above heart level, measured 200 mm. Hg. When the giraffe's head was forcibly lowered the doctors were astonished to find the blood pressure dropped to 175 mm. Hg.

In 1966 three American physiologists, Robert L. Van Citters, William S. Kemper, and Dean L. Franklin, reported on radiotelemetry studies of blood pressure in wild giraffes. With a minimum of confusion and the help of a highly skilled capture team, two adult male giraffes were caught on successive days from different herds near Kiboko in Kenya. Once lassoed from the fast-moving capture vehicle, the giraffes were on the ground, blindfolded and hobbled, in less than two minutes. Local anesthetic was used for the small incision made to insert the blood-pressure transducer in the carotid artery. Wires from the tiny transducer protruded from the sutured wound to connect to a telemetry pack taped around the giraffe's neck. A half hour after capture the giraffes were on their feet, galloping off to rejoin their herds. Subsequently the giraffes were recaptured, the radiotelemetry equipment removed, and the animals released unharmed.

Blood-pressure readings obtained by radiotelemetry were more accurate than the measurements of previous studies, done when giraffes were badly frightened by penning or affected by immobilizing drugs. The blood pressure of a resting giraffe was found to range from 150/105 mm. Hg to 170/110 mm. Hg. Recapture required several minutes of hard running. During the chase the galloping giraffe's blood pressure rose to 230/125 mm. Hg.

Blood pressure in the giraffe is regulated by the

carotid artery wall, thick, elastic, and muscular, which over-
comes the increased pressure caused by the height to which
blood must be raised to reach the head. Each carotid artery
resembles a narrow truncated cone. Large amounts of
elastic tissue invest the lower portion, while higher up
muscle fibers predominate. Another long-necked African
animal, the ostrich, has similarly modified carotid arteries.

Veins also function in the regulation of blood pressure.
The jugular vein, which carries blood away from the brain,
is more than an inch in diameter. It is so large that it has
a collapsed appearance except when the giraffe's head is
lowered. Then blood collects, pressure increases, and the
paired jugular veins distend to act as large reservoirs. Seven
or eight valves, each with two or three cusps, or "teeth,"
line the thick-walled jugular vein. Each of the jugular's
tributaries is also equipped with a set of valves. The valves
hold the blood, preventing its backward flow into the giraffe's head. At the same time the muscular upper portions
of the carotid arteries counteract arterial pressure built up
by gravity. When the giraffe raises its head, returning blood
rushes down through the almost flattened jugular vein into
the precaval vein which collects blood returning to the
heart from anterior portions of the body. A ring of muscle
slows the blood's entry into the right atrium of the heart.

Blood vessels of the long limbs are so modified that a
giraffe never suffers swollen ankles. After a giraffe calf is
born, striking development of musculature occurs in its
limb arteries. Probably this muscularity develops in re-
sponse to hydrostatic pressure. The very thick walls protect
the capillary circulation. The giraffe's leg veins are also
thick and muscular. The lumens, or openings, of both
arteries and veins in the limbs are pinpoint in diameter.

There are other factors that influence blood pressure.
Each time the giraffe breathes, blood pressure rises and

falls some 15 mm. Hg. When the giraffe gallops, the cyclic drop in blood pressure coincides with the impact of its front hoofs. Blood pressure is also affected by volume of blood, about nine or ten gallons in the giraffe.

For an animal its size, the giraffe has a rapid heartbeat. Radiotelemetry heartbeat records range from ninety beats per minute when the giraffe is lying down to 170 beats per minute when it is galloping. Circulation time—the time required for complete circulation of the blood—takes anywhere from eleven to sixteen seconds in the giraffe.

Big-game hunters often reported that giraffes, when shot, bled little. This led to the assumption that giraffes have very thick blood. Actually the viscosity, or thickness, of giraffe blood is 4.9 times that of water, which means that it is not very thick. If giraffes bleed little it may be because their superficial blood vessels are few and the main blood vessels of their limbs lie deep beneath tendons.

Temperature Regulation

Radiotelemetric measurement of the giraffe's deep body temperature shows it to be remarkably stable. A large block of ice on a hot day melts away more slowly than a small block of ice that has a larger surface area. Similarly, the giraffe, a large mammal with relatively small surface area, exhibits what is called "thermal inertia." At low air temperatures its deep body temperature varies only from 37.7 degrees Centigrade to 39.1 degrees Centigrade. In extreme daytime heat or when the giraffe runs, expending energy and storing body heat, body temperature control is relaxed.

Investigating heat storage in running antelopes, physiologists C. Richard Taylor of Harvard University and C. P.

Lyman of the East African Veterinary Research Organization found that the galloping eland, a large antelope, sweats profusely and shows only a slight increase in body temperature. The small Thomson's gazelle, on the other hand, stores large amounts of heat while running. While body temperature and even the temperature of the blood in its carotid artery rise steeply, its brain temperature does not. Brain and body temperatures are independent in the Thomson's gazelle.

The giraffe and the Thomson's gazelle are among the mammals that have a **rete,** a network formed at the base of the skull where the carotid arteries divide into hundreds of small tortuous arteries. These arteries then re-form to carry blood to the brain. The carotid rete lies in a sinus, or cavity, filled with venous blood, the cavernous sinus.

Until recently the function of the giraffe's rete was thought to be blood-pressure regulation. When the giraffe lowered its head, causing a rush of blood to the brain, it was supposed that the many small arteries of the rete expanded into the venous cavity, temporarily reducing pressure. But the giraffe's blood pressure is well regulated by its thick-walled carotid arteries as well as by its valved jugular veins.

Taylor and Lyman believe that the carotid rete in the Thomson's gazelle has a cooling function. Venous blood is cooled by evaporation from the linings of the nasal passage as the animal breathes. This blood drains back through the cavernous sinus surrounding the rete. An exchange of heat takes place between cool venous blood and warm arterial blood on its way from heart to brain. The rete, as a counter-current cooling device, enables the gazelle, and probably the giraffe, to tolerate high body temperatures during running. The rete may also have something to do with the giraffe's ability to tolerate high daytime temperatures and to go without water for varying lengths of time.

Respiration

The large number and small size of the giraffe's red blood cells provide increased surface area for the exchange of gases. In the lungs, the red blood cells give off carbon dioxide and take on a fresh supply of oxygen (external respiration); the oxygen is then carried to the body tissues and exchanged for carbon dioxide (internal respiration).

François LeVaillant, the eighteenth-century French naturalist, once tried, on horseback, to keep up with a running giraffe. His description appears in *Narratives and Adventures of Travellers in Africa* by Charles Williams:

"We galloped after her, and occasionally fired our muskets; but she insensibly gained so much upon us, that, after having pursued her for three hours, we were forced to stop, because our horses were out of breath, and we entirely lost sight of her."

LeVaillant's giraffe was a long-winded individual. When hard pressed at a gallop for any distance, most giraffes become blown.

Because of its long neck the giraffe has a peculiar respiratory problem. The very long windpipe, or trachea, supported along its length by more than a hundred tracheal rings, is a respiratory "dead space." This long trachea must be ventilated. The volume of air that a giraffe inhales and never uses in respiration is about 1.7 liters. To compensate for its respiratory dead space the giraffe has a large lung capacity—forty-seven liters, or about twelve gallons. When breathing normally, a giraffe uses only about one-tenth to one-twelfth of this total lung capacity.

The giraffe has a relatively slow respiratory rate. Standing quietly, it breathes eight to ten times a minute. This reduces the number of times per minute that the long trachea must be filled with air and increases ventilation of the alveoli (terminal air sacs in the lungs).

The giraffe's long trachea may have a cooling function. Physiologists have found that the rhea, a very large, long-necked South American bird, makes use of its trachea, filled with moist air, to cool blood on its way to the brain.

6 Herds and Individuals

Giraffe herds are rather casual; individuals come and go. Consecutive sightings of a giraffe herd almost never record the same constituents. This loose structure is made possible by the giraffe's excellent vision. Sight is the most highly developed of the giraffe's senses. The ability to maintain visual contact, to see other giraffes as far away as a half-mile or more, sometimes makes it difficult to determine whether a giraffe grouping is a herd. Ethologists (animal behaviorists) use the term "social distance" to define the maximum distance between individuals of a species in a group. For giraffe herds the social distance has been estimated at about five hundred yards.

There are accounts of seventy or more giraffes seen together. More usual are smaller-sized herds of the following compositions: females and young animals of both sexes; females and young animals of both sexes accompanied by a mature bull; adult and young males in bull herds or

bachelor groups; mixed herds of males and females and
young of various ages.

Bull giraffes are frequently seen alone, as are female
giraffes. Often it seems that giraffes prefer the company
of their own sex: females group in twos and threes, usually
with calves at their sides; two bulls consort, though seldom
for long, as males travel from herd to herd.

Bull herds, of up to seven giraffes, are of three kinds,

all of them temporary groupings: herds of large bulls; herds in which a large bull appears to have younger males in his care; herds of males too old to be with their mothers and too young to be accepted as adults in mixed herds.

Mixed herds range in size from an association of a bull and a cow to a herd of fifteen bulls and cows of large and medium sizes. There may be a single large bull or as many as eight bulls in a mixed herd. Sometimes it is a female that leads the herd, but it is the largest of the bulls in any mixed herd that is the dominant animal and herdmaster. Within a herd giraffes are individuals. Some are bold, others wary. Anne Innis Dagg, in her study "The Behaviour of the Giraffe in the Eastern Transvaal," observed:

"In a herd of fifteen giraffe that passed my parked car, a big bull led the way and stood nearest the car to watch it, while the rest of the herd circled round behind him. . . . The first in line was fairly bold and chewed and browsed as she walked. The second did not browse but stared at me as she passed, and the third female was very nervous and kept stopping to stare at me and did not browse or chew."

Daily changes occur in the herds as giraffes leave one group to join another. The comings and goings of a bull called Star are chronicled by Anne Innis Dagg:

"He was often present with other males and females but he was sometimes alone or with a group of males. These herds might be large or small. He sometimes led the herd and sometimes brought up the rear but often he paid little or no attention to the other giraffe at all."

For a few weeks Star associated with a herd of females with calves, showing special interest in the mother of the largest calf. Giraffes have no definite breeding season; females may be in heat, or **estrus,** at any time of the year. Presumably it is the restlessness of bulls, looking for estrous females, that leads to the changes in herd composition.

Home Range

The area over which an animal roams in feeding, mating, and rearing its young is called the **home range.** A giraffe's home range is estimated to be an area of forty to fifty square miles. Home ranges of individual giraffes overlap and include those of other giraffes. Within the forty-four square miles of Nairobi National Park in Kenya, there are usually about eighty giraffes at any one time. These giraffes may be any of 241 individuals that wander freely in and out of the park. In Tanzania, Dr. Bernhard Grzimek, director of the Frankfurt Zoo in Germany, and his son Michael counted 837 giraffes in an aerial game census of the 4500 square miles of the Serengeti National Park. As a herd moves slowly through the bush each giraffe walks and browses at its own pace. The herd may average less than one-seventh of a mile an hour and travel less than a mile in a day's time. Giraffes seldom move far unless forced by drought or grass fire.

Camouflage

A giraffe is well camouflaged in the bush. Usually it is a head that sticks out above a thorn tree, or a flicking ear, or the whisk of a tail that betrays a giraffe's presence. Sometimes a spreading acacia screens a giraffe's body from view so that only its legs are visible. This use of a bush or tree may be deliberate. A giraffe in thornbush or light forest can be approached more closely—that is, it has a shorter flight distance—than a giraffe in the open. Kudus and gerenuks are antelopes that also make use of vegetation screens.

Danger

As they browse, giraffes in a herd may feed in very close proximity or in a widely scattered pattern. Each giraffe lowers its head after snatching browse and gazes about. This means security for the herd, for at all times some giraffes are watchful. Danger causes a scattered herd to move together.

When startled, a giraffe holds its head nearly perpendicular. Its nostrils flare, its eyes blaze, and its ears spread stiffly. Standing thus, motionless and staring, is giraffe communication. Or the giraffe may nervously paw the ground. Turning its body at an angle to the disturbance and switching its tail from side to side also functions as a warning signal to others in the herd. Panic is spread when the giraffe snorts in alarm and plunges forward into a gallop. The other giraffes stampede after it.

Browsing

Browsing occupies most of a giraffe's time, especially during early morning and late afternoon.

Sight, smell, and sampling are used in selecting browse. Often a giraffe sniffs at a bush before beginning to feed on it. Smell presumably is important when the giraffe browses at night. Giraffe nostrils are oblique and slit-like. Special muscles enable the giraffe to close its nostrils at will. This protects the sensitive membrane lining the nostrils from painful pricks and tears of thorns.

So adept at browsing is the giraffe that it can hold a branch in its mouth while it pulls off leaves with its tongue.

Usually a branch is grasped by the giraffe's bristly, prehensile lips. Now and again its eighteen-inch-long, slender, gray tongue wraps around a leafy branch and, with a head pull, the leaves are torn off into its mouth. Frequently giraffes share a branch. Pods, fruits, and twigs are also eaten.

In zoos giraffes find other uses for their tongues. They lick stall surfaces, paddock fences, and even keepers' cheeks. Sir Richard Owen, the British anatomist, noted in the *Transactions of the zoological Society of London* (1841): "As the [peacock] was spreading his tail in the sunbeams and curveting in presence of his mate one of the *Giraffes* stooped his long neck, and entwining his flexile tongue round a bunch of the gaudy plumes, suddenly lifted the bird into the air, then giving him a shake, disengaged five or six of the tail-feathers, when down fluttered the astonished peacock and scuffled off with the remains of his train draggling humbly after him." Possibly the green and blue of the peacock's tail tempted the giraffe; for giraffes are known to be able to distinguish such colors as blue, violet, red, orange, yellow, and green.

Giraffe diet is varied. Many different plant species are eaten at various times of the year. Acacias, dry-country trees common in Africa, are the giraffe's favorite browse and supply much of its food. Some kinds have long thorns and spines. The whistling thorn, a giraffe food staple, may gain some protection from its myrmecophytic (ant-sheltering) adaptations. The black hollow galls, which cause this acacia to "whistle in the wind," are home to a particularly unpleasant kind of ant. But it is quite usual to see leaves, twigs, thorns, and galls disappear into a giraffe's mouth. In South Africa an acacia is named for the giraffe, *Acacia giraffae*. Giraffes and other herbivores scatter seeds in their droppings. Seeds of some acacias apparently require passage through a herbivore's digestive tract in order to germinate.

Giraffes are fond of at least a dozen other varieties of food trees. One of these is the strange "sausage tree," which looks just like a tree hung with sausages. Giraffes eat the big sausage-shaped fruits as well as the leaves. As they browse giraffes snatch branches along with leaves and chew them to extract their sap. During dry seasons giraffes spend more time searching for browse and less time resting and ruminating. When foliage food is scarce giraffes feed on bark. Rarely do giraffes eat grass.

Trees and bushes have deep, spreading roots. Those whose shapes shade their own root systems, called "umbrella trees," stay green longer than the grasses and are not dependent on rains. They leaf out before the rains come, perhaps stimulated by intense heat at the end of the dry season.

Elephants and black rhinos and the graceful impalas are browsers too, but they need more water than giraffes do, and they stay fairly near rivers except during the rains. The browsing specialists are three: giraffe, gerenuk—the strange, long-necked antelope that stands up on its hind-legs to browse—and the dik-dik, an antelope only fourteen inches tall. The giraffe's browsing is done from the tops of the acacias down to four feet above the ground. The gerenuk browses up to a height of eight feet. The dik-dik's feeding territory is the tangle of low branches. Other browsers, like the kudus, prefer to feed on steep rocky hill-sides or in gullies, places avoided by giraffe and gerenuk.

On the undersides of some large trees, a conspicuous **browse line** can be seen about sixteen feet above the ground. These trees are "pruned" into hour-glass shapes by giraffes. Heavily browsed bushes are trimmed to egg-shaped contours.

Browsing may, on occasion, be hazardous. Anthony Cullen, Kenya game warden, in his book *Window onto Wilderness*, quotes an entry from the Tanzania Parks archives (1961): "The Warden found an adult giraffe hanging in a tree—quite dead—about eight miles from Klein's Camp [in the Serengeti]. The giraffe had apparently been feeding on this tree, right on the edge of a three-foot drop, and had slipped. His head had caught in the main fork of the tree, and there he died. When first spotted, two lions had started feeding on the hindquarters."

The daily ration of a zoo giraffe is about twenty pounds of alfalfa or clover hay, ten pounds of feeding pellets (dry food especially prepared for hoofed mammals), and five pounds of rolled oats, cut-up apples, carrots, potatoes, cabbage, bread. Bananas, a now-and-then treat, are eaten peel and all.

Water

When droughts occur, giraffes can go without water for three to eight days; according to some reports, even for several months. Because they are less dependent on water than many other animals they roam over larger territories and less often come to water holes, where in dry periods lions concentrate.

At other times of the year, when water is available, giraffes make regular visits to water holes. Their approach, often in herds of five or six, is slow and cautious. They pay little or no heed to wind direction, but each giraffe stands and looks about for as long as five minutes before walking to the edge of the water hole. Obviously it is the danger giraffes associate with water holes that makes them so wary. The flooded areas that serve as watering places during rainy seasons are approached without hesitation.

A giraffe does not wade into the water to get its drink, probably for fear of becoming stuck in the mud. In order to reach water, the giraffe either splays its forelegs or bends its "knees." Its head bobs up and down several times as it prepares to drink. Always the giraffe watches for predators. If startled while drinking, the giraffe snaps its head back and pulls its forelegs under its body. In less than two seconds the giraffe can regain its upright posture.

With upper lip raised and lower lip plunged into the water the giraffe drinks freely. It drinks two or three times, each time raising its head between drinks to look about.

On a cool day a zoo giraffe's thirst is quenched by two and a half gallons of water, while on a very hot day it drinks as much as ten gallons.

Apparently there is security in numbers at water holes. A single giraffe is quick to get its drink and leave, but giraffes in herds often linger and sometimes engage in sparring matches at water holes.

Giraffes cannot swim. Rivers are barriers they do not cross. In West Africa the Niger and Benue river system has long prevented the Nigerian giraffe from crossing south to savanna that would be suitable giraffe habitat. There are reports that giraffes dislike rain and push their heads up into dense acacia foliage to protect their faces from pelting raindrops.

Salt Licks

Salt licks are favorite giraffe gathering places. With forelegs widely splayed or bent, the giraffe fills its mouth with saline earth, then raises its head, getting the salt it craves. Much time is spent around salt licks. Head-slamming duels are waged there, or the giraffes stand about, ruminating.

A mineral deficiency may be the reason that giraffes sometimes pick up and chew on the ends of bones from a carcass or sample stomach contents spilled on the ground at the site of a kill.

Grooming

Giraffes have short, smooth hair, much like a horse's to the touch. They groom themselves by biting and licking. Even a very young giraffe makes unsuccessful grooming attempts. A three-week-old calf may raise a hindfoot, turn its head, then in apparent frustration bite at its forearm. Height and a short-coupled body make it difficult for an adult giraffe to scratch with a hoof. Nibbling with lower incisor teeth relieves itching over most of the giraffe's body—even to back and tail root, which the giraffe reaches with the angle of its mouth. As for the tail itself, when raised to one side it can be nibbled along its length, and its long hairs "combed out" by being pulled through the giraffe's mouth.

The tail, which can reach forward to the giraffe's shoulders, is an effective fly switch. Skin twitching is another way of dislodging insects. Giraffes can twitch the skin over most of their bodies, including the hindquarters.

Much grooming is done by licking. Giraffes lick themselves and others in the herd. To relieve itching they scratch —necks on tree trunks, heads on branches, one leg against

another. To stop the itching on its belly a giraffe may strad-
dle a thorny bush. Termite mounds, satisfactory scratching
posts for other animals, are ignored by giraffes. Oxpeckers
or tick birds perform their service of picking and tugging
at ticks embedded in giraffe hides.

Drowsing

In midday heat giraffes often stand about and appear to
drowse. Their heads are lowered, their necks sag, their
forelegs shift, and their tails switch lazily. Sometimes a
branch or tree fork offers welcome support for the weight
of a giraffe's head. Seldom do giraffes seek shade, perhaps
because they are protected from the sun's rays by the thickness of their hides and by heat reflection from their light-
colored hair.

Lying Down

During this time of reduced activity some of the giraffes in the herd lie down. A giraffe first kneels with its forelegs, then lowers the rest of its body to the ground. Forelegs are tucked up on one side or folded under the body. Usually the neck and head are up as the giraffe chews its cud or snatches leaves from a low bush nearby. Giraffes may stay down, resting, for an hour or more. Because they are especially vulnerable in this position they lie down only when they feel safe.

Sleep

Ruminants sleep now and then and only for short periods. Giraffes in zoos have been observed sleeping—usually lying

down with neck arched back beside the body and head tucked back beside the tail, the lower jaw resting on the hindlegs. A baby giraffe sleeps with its head resting on its back, a pose to delight any artist. A zoo giraffe sleeps perhaps five times during a night for about six or seven minutes at a time. Usually the giraffe has its back against a stall wall. Any unfamiliar sound or light quickly rouses a zoo giraffe.

Getting Up

The giraffe uses its neck to get up. First the neck is drawn back, then thrust forward, as the giraffe gets onto its "knees." In this position another thrust backward, then forward, helps to raise the hindquarters. Then the neck is drawn back a third time to free the forelegs as the giraffe

gets up from its "knees." Once up, the giraffe
stretches, arching its back, extending its neck and
hindlegs, one after another, and switching its tail.

7 Giraffes in Motion

The giraffe's long neck has several uses. It enables the giraffe to browse at tree levels above the reach of other herbivores (although some elephants may reach the same browse levels with their trunks). As a lookout tower for detecting predators the giraffe's head and neck are unsurpassed. But it is when the giraffe moves, especially at the gallop, that its neck performs its most conspicuous function, in fact, the neck is essential to the giraffe's locomotion.

Giraffes in motion have been variously described as "pitching ships" and "rocking horses." In 1840 the British sportsman William Cornwallis Harris, in *Portraits of the Game and Wild Animals of Southern Africa,* wrote of a galloping giraffe:

"Sailing before me with incredible velocity, his long swan-like neck keeping time to the eccentric motion of his stilt-like legs—his ample black tail curled above his back, and whisking in ludicrous concert with the rocking of his disproportioned frame, he glided gallantly along 'like some tall ship upon the ocean's bosom,' and seemed to leave whole leagues behind him at each stride."

Pacing

Much of a giraffe's time is spent moving slowly among scattered trees, searching for browse. At a slow walk, head and neck move forward and back with each step. Moving a bit faster, the giraffe paces. The legs on either side of its body move forward together, as lateral rather than diagonal pairs. Left front and hind hoofs touch the ground at almost the same time. Then the right legs move forward as a pair. The sequence of footfalls when a giraffe paces is left hind, left fore, right hind, right fore.

When a giraffe's pacing walk is analyzed it is seen that during each stride each lateral leg pair is on the ground 40 per cent of the time. Weight is supported first by its left legs and then by its right legs. Side-to-side swaying is controlled by the giraffe's body weight and by lateral inertia due to its body height. A complete stride takes about two seconds. Pacing speed is ten miles an hour, somewhat faster than the trot of an ordinary horse. At the pace, neck and head move back and forth twice during each stride. Forward thrust shifts the center of gravity to the front, helping to move the giraffe's body forward. Just before each lateral pair of hoofs touches ground, the frontal thrust of head and neck is greatest. At this time, the angle between neck and back is greatest. Then, as each lateral hoof pair is set down, the head and neck move back, decreasing the giraffe's forward momentum. In other words, the neck is drawn back as the giraffe begins to move a lateral leg set, and thrust forward as the legs complete the stride.

There are several possible explanations as to why the giraffe paces. By pacing, rather than moving on diagonals, the short-coupled giraffe may overcome the problem of its very long legs interfering. Pacing may enable a greater use of trunk or body musculature and thus the expenditure of less energy. Allowing for longer strides, pacing is a faster gait than the diagonal walk.

The okapi paces too, indicating that this unique gait may have been developed among the prehistoric short-necked giraffes. Comparative studies of the walking gaits of various ruminants indicate that the use of lateral leg support depends primarily upon the anatomy of giraffe and okapi.

Galloping

The giraffe's other gait is the gallop. The neck is thrust forward, the neck-back angle increases from 115 to 165 degrees, and the weight is over the forelegs. Neck movement is more exaggerated in the gallop than the pace.

As the giraffe gallops its neck arches forward, once for each complete stride. With each stride the giraffe pushes off with its hindlegs. Part of the driving force comes from the muscles of its sloping back, but the main propulsion is supplied by its forelegs. The neck's momentum pulls the body forward with each forward thrust. The spread forelegs are carried forward. Then hindlegs move forward outside the forelegs. The four legs come together under the giraffe, and there is a brief interval of flexed suspension when all four hoofs are off the ground. The hoofs make four successive impacts. Hindlegs touch the ground: one, two; then forelegs: three, four. At the end of each stride the neck moves backward, slowing the forward momentum of the body and enabling the giraffe to keep its balance. Each one-second stride covers ten feet or more.

Galloping speeds of giraffes range from fifteen miles an hour for a cow with calf galloping at her side to as fast as forty miles an hour. Several giraffes were clocked at speeds of twenty-eight to thirty-two miles an hour over

a few miles. Such speeds are surprising when the slow rhythms of neck and legs are considered.

Giraffes in motion are incredibly graceful. They gallop with tails twisted up over their backs, possibly to prevent the long-haired tassels from catching on thorns. Their heads duck and swerve to avoid branches. Their forelegs balance their long necks. A. Brazier Howell, an American mammalogist, noted in *Speed in Animals,* "The length and heaviness of the limbs introduce certain requirements in the locomotion of the giraffe that are unique among living mammals. The stride is long and the rhythm slow, partly because this must correspond to the slow rhythm of a long neck. Hence there is some appearance of clumsiness and of the

gaits being labored. Actually, however, slow motion pictures show the giraffe to be one of the most graceful of mammals, surpassing in this respect many of the lighter antelopes."

Jumping

Giraffes are surprisingly good jumpers. Cattle fences, an unfortunate part of the settled African landscape, do not deter giraffes. They have been known to get over wire fences four and a half feet high. Here again the neck is important to the giraffe. At the take-off the neck is pulled back, concentrating weight over the hindlegs, and the giraffe pops its forelegs over the wire strands. Then, with neck thrust forward to shift weight to its front end, the giraffe hauls its hindlegs over the fence.

Sometimes a giraffe calf cannot scramble over a fence that separates it from its mother and the rest of the herd. Eventually the forlorn young animal wanders off on its own.

8 Necking, Sparring, and Fighting

A giraffe uses its neck to express emotions. When standing, the angle of its neck to the ground is usually fifty to sixty degrees. In anger, head and neck are lowered almost to a horizontal position. This is the threat position. To express submission a giraffe stretches its neck and raises its nose in the air.

Necking, sparring, and fighting are restricted to male giraffes in bull herds. **Head-slamming** matches establish the hierarchy, or ranking order, of physical and sexual dominance, and serious battles are avoided.

Nonchalantly one bull approaches another until only four or five yards separate them. Proudly the challenger postures, legs and neck held rigid, his flexed shoulder turned toward his opponent. This is met by a similar display. The two bulls move in a peculiar stiff-legged fashion. They

stand close together, head to head, their forelegs in firmly straddled stances. They lean heavily on each other, pressing shoulders or flanks as though testing each other's strength. Then one of the giraffes, usually the larger, lowers his head, curves it to the outside and swings it at his opponent. His neck swings high, rubbing against the other bull's neck. The neck-rubbing head-swings continue until one giraffe loses interest and wanders off, or the necking may lead to sparring.

When sparring, giraffes take a firmer, straddled position. Rhythmically they swing their necks to the side and slightly backward to deliver loud blows against each other's necks. The blows are parried—each giraffe tries to dodge his opponent's head-slams. With each blow, one bull's horns, worn hairless at the top from previous contests, jab at the underside of the other's neck and shoulders. Between bouts one or both giraffes may displace by snatching browse from a nearby bush.

Usually necking and sparring take place between two male giraffes, but three or four males have been seen lining up to take head-swinging turns. Even young male giraffes take part in head-slamming sessions. In her study of the behavior of the giraffe, Anne Innis Dagg mentions that she saw a young male sparring between two large bulls. "They hit him gently from both sides, and the baby between them waved his head about in all directions, sometimes completely missing both of them."

Between two large, equally matched, mature bulls head-slamming is serious fighting. Even when a herd with female giraffes is in the vicinity the males carry on their head-slamming sessions. The bulls stand in head-to-tail position, their forelegs splayed wide apart. One giraffe rubs his neck along the back and flanks of the other. Soon their necks are swinging across each other's backs, their heads twisted so that their horns strike each other's sides.

During a fight giraffes sometimes wrap their necks together. They shove and push. Then they circle and resume head-hitting. Their horns jab at loins and flanks, frequently causing the giraffes to become sexually aroused. After a bout a giraffe may try to mount his opponent or another bull in the herd.

Sooner or later the loser withdraws. The winner, with head raised, pursues only a short distance. In one instance, however, an unfortunate giraffe, retreating in defeat, got hung up on a wire fence. The victor pursued him and slammed mercilessly at his unprotected hindquarters.

The force of giraffe head blows is great. In Kruger National Park a giraffe bull, knocked out by another bull's head-slam, lay unconscious for some twenty minutes. A bull named Otto at the Frankfurt Zoo, pestered beyond endurance by a large male eland, took a powerful head swing. The thousand-pound eland was tossed through the air to land with a broken shoulder.

The giraffe's blunt horns are well suited for its stylized fighting technique. Nevertheless injury is sometimes inflicted. An entry in the archives of the Kenya Parks notes that an old male giraffe was killed by another giraffe in a battle that lasted for about half an hour.

9 Courtship, Reproduction, and Birth

Giraffes are sexually mature when they are three to four years old. Female giraffes mature somewhat earlier than males. Once a cow attains sexual maturity she comes into heat every twelve to fifteen days. Unlike most ungulates, giraffes breed throughout the year. This means that there is no definite calving season, although in different parts of Africa there appear to be seasonal peaks.

Two unusual behavior patterns are associated with mating in giraffes, **flehmen** and use of the **leg beat.** Flehmening, which occurs when an animal finds an interesting smell, is done by almost all ungulate species except members of the pig family, whose snout structure makes this impossible. Among giraffes flehmening is a male prerogative, quite different from the urine licking that is done by giraffes of both

76

sexes, young and old. A male giraffe, on joining a herd, flehmens the urine of the females. This he does by approaching a cow and pushing his nose against her hindquarters or licking or nibbling her tail, inducing the cow to urinate. The bull collects some of the urine with his tongue, then extends his head and holds it motionless for a minute or two. His upper lip curls upward. This closes off his nostrils, trapping odors in the nasal cavity where they can be thoroughly assessed by the olfactory epithelium, or smell-sensitive lining. The bull may eject the urine from his mouth

in a long stream. Presumably, in flehmening, bull giraffes test for cows in heat, by detecting hormone-content changes in urine samples. If a cow is not in heat the bull loses interest and wanders off.

Usually a bull is tolerant of other bulls, allowing them to flehmen the cows in his herd. Now and then, grunting as he gallops, a bull chases younger bulls a short distance off from the herd. But a dominant bull, the high carriage of his head indicating his social position in the herd, is not always tolerant. Although he pays little attention to younger bulls, he will approach a mature bull intruder to start a sparring or fighting contest, or he will trot toward the new-comer and, with legs stiffened, posture. More often than not the other bull changes his mind about joining the herd.

Use of the leg beat in giraffe courtship occurs when a bull closely follows a cow that is in heat. When she stops, the bull raises a foreleg and taps it against the cow's hindleg. If she does not move off the bull attempts mounting. Or the bull may test the cow's readiness for mating by resting his head against her flank. If she canters off the bull usually persists. Often a bull follows a cow for hours before successful mating takes place. Mating is brief but repeated a number of times within a several-hour period.

Fourteen to fifteen months after mating a baby giraffe is born. Single births are the rule. In most instances the "twins" that appear in giraffe herds are youngsters of the same age.

However, it is possible that giraffes sometimes produce twins. A game warden in a Kenya park made note of the fact that a very light-colored cow giraffe was seen with two identical calves of the same color when there were no other giraffes in the vicinity. An actual record of giraffe twinning comes from the San Francisco Zoo, where twin calves were stillborn in 1943. Sex ratios at birth favor male giraffes (61.5 per cent).

Giraffe births have frequently been observed in zoos. Usually anxiety is the first sign that parturition, or birth, is underway. The cow paces nervously and eats little. Hours later the calf's forefeet protrude from her birth canal. Its small hoofs are covered with jellylike pads that prevent tearing of the membranes that surround its body. During labor the cow moves about restlessly. With each contraction she spreads her hindlegs and extends her head and neck. Now and again she lies down, then gets up. As the cow strains, the calf is slowly pushed out into the world. Its head lies along its outstretched forelegs. Cephalic, or head-first, presentation is normal in giraffes and all other mammals that have comparatively small heads and necks and comparatively rigid hindquarters. The fetal membranes have burst, and the calf's tongue and lips move, but it still "breathes" through its placental attachment to the cow.

About forty minutes after its front hoofs appear the giraffe calf is dropped—quite literally, falling five and a half feet to the ground. Zookeepers are careful to see that a cow's stall is deeply covered with straw so that the newborn calf will not be injured on arrival and will have good footing. When the calf is expelled the umbilical cord, containing the blood vessels that connect fetus with mother during the calf's development in the uterus, ruptures. Now the calf breathes on its own. The cord's twelve-inch remnant may dangle from the calf's belly for two months before dropping off.

The giraffe cow turns to look at her newborn calf. She appears nervous. The calf struggles free of the membranes. Feebly it raises its head and neck. The cow, with forelegs widely spread, lowers her head and begins to lick the calf's nose, eyes, and head. She takes each ear into her mouth with a sucking motion. At first the baby tries to avoid her long tongue.

In captivity the process of a giraffe's birth takes anywhere from twenty minutes to several hours. Birth in the
wild usually is a shorter process. It is a time of danger for
the giraffe, as it is for all hoofed mammals. Hyenas often
lurk nearby.

In Kruger National Park, Dr. Grzimek happened upon
a giraffe giving birth. In his book *Among Animals of Africa*,
he noted that ". . . no less than nine giraffes formed a circle
round the expectant mother. . . . The calf succeeded in
standing after about ten minutes but fell over again. These
exertions were repeated over a period of some twenty-five
minutes, after which time the young giraffe walked round
its mother and seemed quite strong. All the other giraffes
bent to nuzzle the new addition to the herd."

The giraffe gesture of nuzzling is a **tactile encounter,** used to examine a new giraffe. Giraffes frequently nose one another's body, neck, or head. Sometimes a giraffe licks another's neck, mane, horns, or eyes, or it may rub its head against another giraffe, or its leg against the body of a giraffe that is lying down.

Thirty minutes to an hour after its birth the calf is on its feet. Rather unsteadily it searches for the cow's swollen milk bag. It tries to suckle on its mother's "knee." Finally the calf locates one of the four teats. It suckles eagerly, for as long as ten minutes this first time.

Colostrum, or the mother's first milk, is vital to the calf. In it are antibodies that protect the newborn animal from infections. This fact was learned after numerous unsuccessful attempts to hand-rear zoo-born calves. Now when a cow refuses to let her newborn calf suckle, zoo men know that colostrum is essential and that the orphan calf must be kept in very clean, isolated quarters. Colostrum from a dairy cow can replace that of the giraffe; it is bottle-fed to the calf for the first forty-eight hours, supplemented by antibiotic injections. After this a commercial formula is substituted for giraffe milk.

It may be ten hours after birth before the cow expels the placenta, the vascular structure through which the calf received oxygen and nutriment from its mother during its fetal life. The cow will only sniff at the placenta. In the wild it is food for waiting hyenas or jackals. By this time the calf can run at its mother's side.

During the first two days of a calf's life its mother follows its every move. After the second day there is a change —the calf follows its mother.

10 The Calf

At birth a giraffe calf is about six feet tall (top of head) and weighs between 100 and 150 pounds. Its proportions are less exaggerated than those of an adult giraffe. Its upright, S-shaped neck is shorter. The bristly mane runs down onto its back and sometimes has an extension on the rump. Two horn cartilages, flat-lying to facilitate the calf's birth, can be felt under the skin on the head. Each is topped by a tuft of black hair. During the first days of the calf's life the horns actually move about on the skull, to which they are attached only by connective tissue. Very soon the horns become erect, as bone begins to replace cartilage. The calf's short hair has a woolly texture. On each flank a spiral hair tract or whorl is conspicuous. Giraffes have no inguinal fold, the skin-fold connecting flank and hindquarters.

Spots of calves tend to be paler than those of older giraffes, and, permanent though these spots are, they may change shape as the calf grows. Often a calf's spots have

pale centers, while spots of older giraffes may have dark central streaks. Pigmentation, or the deposition of color, apparently occurs in the center of each spot and expands. A giraffe fetus at eight months is fully haired but there is no indication of spotting. So it is after this time that the developing calf acquires its spots. At least three giraffe calves have been born without spots. Two of the spotless giraffes, sisters, are in the Ueno Zoo in Tokyo, Japan.

A calf's background color tends to be lighter than its mother's. With age it darkens. From each "knee" a black stripe runs down the front of the calf's cannon bone. This stripe, reminiscent of the okapi's persistent foreleg stripe, fades as the calf grows and is barely visible in the adult.

No young animal is more charming than a giraffe calf. A two-week-old orphan Masai giraffe that I met on Crescent Island in Kenya's Lake Naivasha was the very picture of self-possession. A farmer had found this little giraffe, named Twiga (Swahili for giraffe), caught in a wire fence and brought it to the island sanctuary, where it roamed free, in the care of an African boy. Twiga was unperturbed by five small lion cubs and a tame bull eland that also lived on the island. Two ostriches became Twiga's special friends. Mildly curious about people, the calf came up to have its neck stroked. Then, after a few minutes, it turned to follow Kinua, the African boy.

Curiosity is characteristic of young giraffes. Even a chameleon in a bush is noticed. More than one observer of a giraffe herd has found himself being stared at by an inquisitive calf. Often the young animal disappears, only to reappear from another direction for a closer look.

A young giraffe is by no means tied to its mother's apron strings. The parental bond is loose. Calves enjoy their own company in the herd. Much of the time the calves are together, browsing from the same bush or lying down close

beside one another. At times they are playful and gallop about, frisking and bucking. A tired calf flops to the ground; minutes later it is up again. Frequently the calves wander off as far as a hundred yards from the herd, but almost always they are within visual-contact distance of the adult giraffes.

In the social organization of giraffe herds **nurseries** are provided for the very young calves. Giraffes, and certain other hoofed mammals, maintain a "baby-sitting" or "auntie" arrangement in which one or two cows look after all the calves. The "aunties" may be old females, beyond the age of calf-bearing. While they stay with the nursery group, the mother giraffes browse some distance away. C. A. W. Guggisberg, a naturalist who lives in Kenya, wrote in his book *Giraffes*, ". . . these nurseries form and break up as casually as all other giraffe groupings. The calves are still being suckled and therefore dependent on their mothers; they are simply being looked after while most of the females have wandered off in the seemingly aimless manner so characteristic of the species."

Usually there are five or six calves in a nursery, rarely as many as twelve. Within the nursery there is much activity. Two calves swing their heads and necks in play; another calf is curious about a bat-eared fox that skulks behind a whistling thorn. The small fox, a nighttime hunter, was lying near the entrance of its burrow, sunning, until the giraffes appeared.

Four to eight times a day the zoo-born giraffe calf suckles. Its mother's milk, at first rich and concentrated, has changed to one-third its original fat content and one-half the protein content, but lactose (a form of sugar) is increased. At two to three weeks the giraffe calf begins to supplement its milk diet with leaves. By the time it is several months old the calf is quite self-sufficient. Cud-chewing commences during its fourth month, but for nearly a year

the calf will suckle. Sometimes, when it has started to suckle, other calves and even adults sample the mother giraffe's milk. As long as her calf suckles the cow tolerates the others.

During its first year a giraffe calf grows rapidly, adding more than three feet to its stature. Although growth continues until it is seven or eight years old, full height is reached by the giraffe's fourth year. For females this is about fourteen feet, for males about seventeen feet. Weight for adult giraffes averages nearly eighteen hundred pounds. In the wild, a very large bull may weigh about three thousand pounds or more.

Giraffe death rates are highest during the first year of life, when more than half the calves born may not survive. Predation takes a relatively small toll among adult giraffes. The record life span for a zoo giraffe is twenty-eight years. Giraffes in the wild have lived as long as twenty-six years. Fifteen to twenty years is a more usual giraffe life span.

11 Giraffes and Other Animals

Giraffes like company. Zebras, elands, and harte-beests are their frequent associates. In northern Kenya the large-eared Grevy's zebras share the reticulated giraffes' habitat. Possibly the zebras feel secure when they have the long-necked giraffes nearby as lookout towers. When giraffes show alarm, panic spreads instantly to whatever animals are about—zebras, rhinos, buffaloes, hartebeests, wildebeests, elands, impalas, or gazelles.

Occasionally a large bull giraffe is the companion of one or two old rogue elephants. Schillings, in 1906 was the first to record this association. For eight days he followed such a trio in the bush. Old elephants probably derive peace of mind when they have a giraffe sentry; and in heavy bush, where it is hard to see any distance, the giraffe

94

may benefit from the elephants' ability to detect danger by their sense of smell. However it is, the companions travel together, snatching at browse from the same nose-tip level. Possibly they share a bond, these animals with their very different solutions—long neck and long trunk—to the problem of reaching high for food. Sometimes solitary old bull giraffes are seen in the company of wildebeests, zebras, or ostriches.

Giraffes are quick to join other giraffes in galloping, even when the frightened herd is as far as a mile away. But a herd of buffaloes, galloping in the distance, arouses only their curiosity. When hartebeests and zebras, some three hundred yards away, bolt in alarm, giraffes will spook and follow, or they may stand and watch.

Where there are cattle ranches giraffes have learned to drink at water troughs. Usually they avoid the cattle. But an old bull giraffe in the Transvaal herded a harem of sixty domestic cows. He drove off the domestic bulls. This arrangement lasted for a month. For a time he was joined by two other giraffes. Then all three giraffes left the cows.

Tick birds (red-billed and yellow-billed oxpeckers) often accompany giraffes. Sometimes as many as twelve cling to a giraffe's neck and flanks. Their shrill, chattering calls may alert a resting giraffe, but as sentries they are probably of little importance to giraffes, whose lookout-tower vision is far more efficient at predator detection. For many other large mammals the birds are indispensable. When their alarm calls fail to excite a buffalo or a rhino the birds hammer away at the animal's head. So persistent are tick birds that one was seen trying to rouse, by frantic pecking, a rhino that had been shot.

Tick birds wait in trees near water holes or streams. When animals come to drink they fly down to search for parasites. This is most annoying to a giraffe. When its head is lowered for a drink the birds hop down its neck and peck away inside its sensitive ears. Vigorous head shakes, with ears flapping and eyes closed, dislodge the birds only momentarily. As soon as the giraffe lowers its head to drink again the birds are back.

Relatives of the starling, tick birds have sharp, curved claws. They climb all over giraffes, up and down their legs, over their backs, and under their bellies. They carry on their mating displays and sunbathe as they are carried about on giraffe backs. Long, stiff-feathered tails support the birds as they cling to a giraffe's sides, searching its hide for ticks.

When a tick is found the bird pecks or pulls at it, sometimes working its laterally flattened beak in scissors fashion. Tick-bird food comes from the blood the tick has sucked as well as any blood-sucking flies the birds snatch. If a giraffe has a skin wound the tick birds aggravate it by their incessant pecking. They help themselves to blood from the sore and eat bits of tissue. This unpleasant habit prevents healing and keeps the tick birds supplied with maggots that hatch after flies lay eggs in the open sores. Tick birds also help themselves to giraffe hairs, which they use to line their nests. In South Africa, buffalo weavers take the tick birds' place.

Giraffes sometimes carry piapiacs on their necks or backs. These all-black, magpie-like birds use the giraffes as moving perches from which to snatch insects that hop or fly out of the giraffe's way. Buff-backed herons, sometimes called cattle egrets, often keep abreast of giraffe forelegs, snapping up insects that spring out of the giraffe's path.

12 Predators and Man

 Predators add tension to the African scene. They maintain an intricate system of checks and balances that keeps prey populations within bounds imposed by the environment. They weed out animals in poor condition, thus keeping the herds healthy. To watch giraffes or any of the hoofed mammals come to a water hole is to feel this tenseness. Muscles are taut; expressions are alert. These are animals that must be swift to avoid a predator's stealth and cunning.

Because of their size giraffes have some immunity from predation, an immunity they share with elephant, hippo, and rhino. But lions do kill giraffes, so, like any prey animal, the giraffe must know the lion's potential.

Giraffes pay little attention to a lion that strolls in the open, perhaps seventy yards away. Because of their ability to defend themselves against attacking lions, giraffes have a flight distance that is considerably lower than the flight distances of zebras and gazelles. They allow a predator to approach to within twenty or thirty yards before galloping off. George B. Schaller, an American ethologist, spent three years studying lions in the Serengeti. His observations indicate that the hoofed mammals recognize the lion's relative lack of speed and its need to approach closely, before its intended prey can attain full running speed. It is the lion that creeps, belly to the ground, through tall grass, freezing whenever its intended prey spots it, that giraffes instinctively fear; or the lion that hides in dense cover along streams when dry-season fires have burned off all other stalking cover. Giraffes and other prey animals stay away from dense vegetation and usually come to drink in daylight.

Schaller listed nine giraffes killed or scavenged by lions in three years, as compared to 409 wildebeests, 255 zebras, and 331 Thomson's gazelles. On the ten occasions that he saw lions pursue giraffes the stalks or chases were unsuccessful. Another study in the Serengeti over an eight-year

period records six observations of lion-killed giraffes. Of 128 kills tallied in southern Kenya and central Tanzania, six giraffe kills represent 4 per cent, while wildebeests account for 49 per cent, zebras 15 per cent, Thomson's gazelles 10 per cent, and buffaloes and impalas each 5 per cent. In Kruger Park thirty-one giraffes were killed by lions in one year.

Indolent by day, lions lie about in the shade or drape

themselves on the boulders of kopjes, the islands of rocks that dot areas of the Serengeti. In other parts of Africa lions stretch out on branches of fig trees or yellow-barked fever trees. By late afternoon lions rouse themselves to become watchful of prey species. Most of their hunting is done at dusk and during night. Darkness favors the lion, for then a giraffe's safety depends upon its hearing and smell instead of its sight.

Hunts are often cooperative ventures in which two or more lions take part. The hunt begins with a search. Scanning the area, the lions sit or walk slowly with their heads extended. Spotting a prey animal (or group of animals), the big cats gaze intently. Sometimes they fan out: the lions in the center lie down or creep forward, bodies pressed to the ground, while those at the flanks walk forward. Now and then their tails twitch. Stalking may be a slow forward movement or the technique of stalk and freeze. Then comes the run. The lions chase at speeds of up to thirty miles an hour. When the run is successful a forepaw grabs the prey from the side or behind. With one paw on the back and the other on the flank or chest of the prey, the lion (or sometimes two lions) topples its prey. Biting at the throat usually causes a large prey animal's death by strangulation; less often death results from suffocation as a lion seizes its prey by the muzzle.

An adult-giraffe kill may last a pride of eleven lions three days. But hunting giraffes is not without risk to the lions. In his book *Downey's Africa* Cullen noted: "When circling vultures and hyena moving about prompted an investigation, this led to an area that was beaten flat in some tremendous struggle. In the center of it all was an enormous bull giraffe, with tracks of lion all around. The giraffe was quite dead, and a full-grown lioness was pinned beneath one great shoulder, crushed completely flat."

More often it is young giraffes that lions kill. Once the kill is made, the mother giraffe may stay close by, chasing away hyenas that hope to share the kill.

Of more than a thousand stalking lions observed by Schaller, only 3 per cent were males. Never was a male lion seen assisting in driving or ambushing of prey, but male lions are opportunists, quick to respond to the unexpected. Guggisberg, in *Giraffes*, wrote of a kill by a single male lion in the Masai Amboseli Game Reserve. "I was at Ol Tukai Camp when a big male lion accounted for an adult giraffe on the edge of Loginya Swamp, only a short distance from the game warden's house. . . . This happened at night and the lion remained on the kill for several days, roaring furiously whenever other lions appeared in the vicinity." In Nairobi National Park a large bull Masai giraffe that lost his footing on a rocky slope, stumbling or slipping up behind, was ambushed and killed by a lion. Surprise was on the side of these lions—at the swamp and on the rocky hillside.

Surprise also was on the side of a lion-giraffe struggle described in verse more than a hundred years ago by Thomas Pringle, a settler in South Africa, and published in Charles Williams' *Narratives and Adventures of Travellers in Africa*:

> The tall giraffe stoops down to drink:
> Upon him straight the savage springs
> With cruel joy!—The desert rings
> With clanging sound of desperate strife—
> The prey is strong and strives for life.
> Now plunging tries with frantic bound,
> To shake the tyrant to the ground—
> He shrieks—he rushes through the waste
> With glaring eyes and headlong haste.
> In vain!—the spoiler on his prize
> Rides proudly—tearing as he flies.

For life the victim's utmost speed
Is mustered in this hour of need;
For life—for life—his giant might
He strains, and pours his soul in flight;
And, mad with terror, thirst and pain,
Spurns with wild hoof the thundering plain.

It is doubtful that a giraffe ever gallops far with an attacking lion on its back. Such water-hole ambushes often end in the giraffe's escape. The lion leaps at the giraffe from behind, but the giraffe's violent kicks force it to let go. Long, raking scars on the hindquarters of some giraffes are evidence of such close calls.

A giraffe's defense, when it cannot flee, is to strike out with its forefeet or turn and kick with its hindfeet. On occasion these chopping blows and powerful kicks have killed adult lions. Sometimes a giraffe strikes at a human being. Theodore Roosevelt, twenty-sixth president of the United States, once provoked a giraffe. As leader of an expedition in 1909, Roosevelt was stalking reticulated giraffes along the Uaso Nyiro River in Kenya when he came upon a large cow, her head thrust among the branches of a tall acacia, eyes closed and apparently dozing. Roosevelt walked to within ten feet of the giraffe. Suddenly she reacted, pouting her lips, rearing and striking with a foreleg. Her flailing hoof just missed the intrepid TR. Then, indifferently, the giraffe turned and walked away.

A giraffe cow vigorously defends her calf. For protection the calf gallops to its mother and backs underneath her belly. The calf's body is at right angles to its mother's, its head turned to watch the predator. Unless the cow becomes frantic this position protects her calf and leaves striking room for her forefeet. In one instance a cheetah threatened a baby giraffe, only to be driven off by the fury of the

mother giraffe. Frederick Courtenay Selous, a British big-game hunter famous for his travels in Africa in the late nine-teenth century, saw a newborn giraffe calf lying in the grass suddenly attacked by two leopards. The cow rushed at the leopards, striking with her forefeet. The leopards retreated, but not before a blow from the mother's front hoof had landed on her calf, breaking its back. Selous and his men were forced to end the calf's suffering with a bullet.

Leopard attacks on giraffes are rare. Dense cover is essential, for a leopard usually hunts alone, stalking its prey or springing from ambush, and giraffes, especially cows with calves, avoid forested areas. Because a leopard weighs only 120 pounds it usually cannot prey on large animals. However, a bull giraffe, captured and moved into a Kenya game reserve, wandered over to browse on a tree when

suddenly a leopard sprang from a branch. The giraffe's neck was so badly mauled that it died. Hyenas and wild dogs are also suspected killers of young giraffes, although actual sight records are lacking.

Crocodiles will seize and eat anything they can. The huge reptiles are threats to all animals that come to drink at streams and pools. Occasionally a full-grown giraffe is seized, pulled into the water, and drowned by a crocodile.

As for giraffes and snakes, an unusual incident was reported by George Adamson, for many years a game warden in Kenya. He came upon a dead giraffe lying on top of a dead python. Apparently the python had coiled itself around the giraffe's neck, strangling it, and then the giraffe's body weight had pinned the snake to the ground.

Of all the giraffe's enemies man is the most dangerous. From prehistoric times he has hunted giraffes. Northern African rock engravings and paintings, six to seven thousand years old, attest man's use of snares and traps, spears and poisoned arrows. Giraffe trophies have always been prized. More than three thousand years ago the Egyptian boy king Tutankhamon received the tail of a giraffe as one of his coronation gifts. Africans weave the black tail hairs into arm bands or loop them as necklaces. Fly switches are made of giraffe tail hairs. In South Africa thirty-foot-long whip lashes for ox teams were once made from single strips of the thick, tough hide. Giraffe hide is used to make sandals, shields, and drums. Tendons of giraffe leg muscles are used for sewing and for stringing musical instruments. To native hunters giraffe meat is a feast.

With guns came the relentless killing of giraffes as well as other game animals. Giraffes became extremely shy. Seventy years ago, in his book *In Wildest Africa*, Schillings expressed apprehension about the giraffe: "This wonderful and harmless animal is being completely annihilated. . . .

The day cannot be far distant when the beautiful eyes of the last Twiga will close forever on the desert." Fortunately Schillings was not alone in his concern. Sportsmen began to lose their enthusiasm for hunting giraffes. Professional hunters who killed for hides were denounced. Giraffes gained protection from man just in time.

Twenty-five years after Schillings' ominous warning the *Journal of Mammalogy* printed these words by Herbert Friedmann, an American ornithologist returned from Africa: "One morning as I looked out of my tent towards the mountain the heads of two giraffes serenely contemplating me from over an acacia tree were silhouetted against the rosy cone of Kibo [the higher of Mount Kilimanjaro's two peaks] and as day approached the silhouette gradually changed into colored reality. For over twenty minutes those two stood there watching me, and when they finally ambled off I left, thankful that public opinion was in their favor and would preserve them for future travellers to gaze upon."

Today in Africa's national parks and game reserves safari-goers in Land Rovers and minibuses do just this, and giraffes are stalked with cameras and not guns. Often it is possible to get within four or five yards of the towering animals.

Sometimes in Africa giraffes as well as other animals must be caught and transported from farmland, where they damage crops, to game reserves or national parks.

One method of capturing giraffes is to lasso them. The capture team pursues a galloping giraffe. As their vehicle speeds alongside the herd the men ready a pole that is fitted with a rope noose. They will attempt to slip the noose over the giraffe's head, or around a hindfoot at the moment it is off the ground. They succeed! Quickly the giraffe is brought to a halt. Although the chase has been brief the giraffe's sides heaved. With another pole the men raise a blanket over

the giraffe's head. Sometimes a bag is used. This blindfold quiets the giraffe.

A harness is placed over the animal's shoulders. The girth is tightened. Three guide ropes are attached. With these the men lead the giraffe toward a holding pen. Once settled in the pen the giraffe gazes placidly over the top rails. Then the team sets off to capture another giraffe. This is soon accomplished. Blindfolds and the harness with guide ropes are used to move the giraffes, one at a time, from the holding pen to the truck. Giraffes travel more easily and quietly in pairs. The men tie leafy branches to the side of the truck so that the giraffes can browse. Canvas covers the top and front of the truck pen, for protection against heat, rain, and wind. Along the route the truck stops several times so that telephone wires can be raised to allow head room for the giraffes. After their journey the giraffes are released and wander slowly off into their new home.

Another capture method is the stockade. Rounded up by men on horseback, a giraffe herd is galloped toward converging "wings" of thornbush that lead into a stockade. Unless the herd's bull leader crashes through the thornbush barricade to freedom, the giraffes are chased into the stockade. With attention and feeding, giraffes tame down in a few days.

Immobilizing drugs are also used to capture giraffes. Once darted, a giraffe soon begins circling movements. Only sufficient dosage to disorient the animal is given—just enough to make it walk in circles. Then the giraffe is easily caught by holding a soft rope at chest height between two groups of men. The giraffe walks into the rope, which is quickly crossed around its hindlegs. Often a rope on one leg is enough to stop a large bull that has been immobilized.

13 Parasites, Diseases, and Injury

Ticks of some fifteen kinds burrow into giraffe hides to feed on blood. Flukes, tapeworms, and whipworms are among the internal pests that live in giraffe intestines. A warble fly, appropriately named *Rhinoestrus giraffae*, lays its eggs on giraffes. After hatching, the parasitic maggots that are the fly's larvae burrow into the delicate lining of the giraffe's nose and throat.

Giraffes are annoyed by swarms of flies, including tsetse flies, carriers of the trypanosomes, which are parasitic protozoans (one-celled animals) that cause trypanosomiasis. African sleeping sickness is one type of trypanosomiasis. The tsetse fly, readily identified by its overlapping wings and stinging bite, picks up the parasite from the blood of an infected animal, wild or domestic. The parasite passes through the fly's gut, multiplying along the way, and enters the salivary glands. With the next bite the tsetse fly transmits the parasite into the bloodstream of another host. Like other African wild animals, giraffes are immune to trypano- somiasis; domestic animals and man are not, a fact that helps to preserve large stretches of grassland and savanna in their natural state.

Rinderpest is an infectious and often fatal disease of ruminants, especially cattle. Cattle imported into Egypt brought rinderpest to Africa. During the 1890s it spread down along cattle trade routes through Kenya and into South Africa. The Masai and other tribes lost most of their cattle herds. Then the disease spread to wild animals, first to buffaloes, elands, and warthogs. Giraffes are less susceptible than many ruminants to rinderpest, but when they are afflicted they often become temporarily blind in one or both eyes and fall easy prey to predators. In 1960 rinderpest took a heavy toll in northern Kenya: 40 per cent of the giraffes died of the disease. Giraffes are also affected when there are outbreaks of anthrax, a bacterial disease, or epidemics of gastroenteritis.

A zebra, wildebeest, or gazelle weakened by injury is soon run down by predators. But giraffes and other large animals may suffer from wounds. Often these are raking lion-claw marks that, covered with flies and maggots and irritated by oxpeckers, cause intense pain.

The First World War brought death to large numbers of giraffes, even though Africa was far away from the armies that battled in Europe. Both Great Britain and Germany had colonies in Africa. Troops were stationed and camps set up along their borders. Sometimes there were skirmishes between the troops, but these did not affect giraffes. What did affect them were the telephone and telegraph wires the

armies set up for communication. Tall poles and high-slung wires appeared for the first time on the African plains.

Giraffes are skillful in dodging tree branches. Galloping fast through the bush, their heads are carried low and their long necks swerve gracefully. However, sauntering across the plains, giraffes hold their heads high. As a result, they collide with unseen wires. Cables burst, poles fall, and giraffes gallop off in terror.

Once the armies discovered that giraffes, not "the enemy," had destroyed their communications, orders went out to shoot giraffes on sight.

Troops were not alone in complaining about giraffes. In the early 1900s A. Blayney Percival, a British game ranger, received frequent messages from the Kenya government's telegraph offices. One, quoted in his *Game Ranger's Note Book*, read: "Either you must keep your giraffe off the lines or we shall have to raise them." Quick to agree to this solution, Percival pointed out that his game department could not be expected to shorten its giraffes.

Giraffes have been victims of trains on the Uganda Railway, which runs from Mombasa on the Indian Ocean to Lake Victoria. Sometimes they are struck by cars. A giraffe that narrowly escapes being hit on the road at night may turn and batter the car with its heels.

14 The Okapi – Close Relatives of Giraffes

In 1871 Sir Henry Morton Stanley, journalist and explorer, made his first and most famous trek to Africa. He was sent by the *New York Herald* to search for the lost missionary, Dr. David Livingstone. Livingstone, seeking to end the slave trade, had disappeared into the bush three years earlier. As everyone knows, Stanley found Dr. Livingstone. Subsequently Stanley devoted many years to exploring the African continent. He was the first white man to learn of the okapi, though he never saw the animal. The Mbuti, people of the Ituri Forest, told Stanley of a creature they called "atti," or donkey, that they sometimes caught in pitfalls.

The second clue to the okapi's existence came from belts made of black-and-white-striped hide worn by forest-dwelling tribesmen. These waistbands were first assumed to be zebra skin, which the Mbuti had got by trade from grassland-dwelling tribes.

In 1899 Sir Harry Johnston, a man of many talents, became governor of the Uganda Protectorate. Before he left England to assume his new post, Johnston talked with Stanley about the "donkey" of the Mbuti. Johnston recalled a book he had once read containing a description of a "unicorn that lived in Equatorial Africa." He was greatly intrigued by the possibility of finding this mysterious animal in the Congo forest.

The vast Ituri Forest, dense, damp, and dark, lies in the northeast corner of the Zaïre Republic (as the Congo is now called), almost at the center of the map of Africa. Small people, the Mbuti, live in camps in forest clearings. Their beehive-shaped huts are made of bent saplings thatched with broad leaves. Silently and swiftly the Mbuti roam through the forest. They hunt the forest animals with nets, spears, bows and arrows, and gather the forest's abundant wild fruits.

A band of these Pygmies was kidnaped in 1900 to be shipped to France for the Paris World Fair. When the smugglers and their captives were halted in Uganda, Johnston himself decided to accompany the Pygmies on their return to the Congo. During the long journey he learned more about a zebralike animal, the "o'api," which had a dark body and more than one hoof on each foot.

When they reached Beni in the Congo, officers stationed at the fort told Johnston of an animal with big ears and slender muzzle that they believed to be a kind of horse. From "askaris," or soldiers, Johnston purchased two striped bandoliers, said to be made of "o'api" skin.

With a few Pygmies as his guides, Johnston pushed deep into the Ituri Forest, determined to find this animal. Hoofprints of the "o'api," clearly showing two toes on each foot, were pointed out to him, but the animal itself was not to be seen. Johnston, more mystified than ever, returned to Uganda, after securing promises from the officers at Beni to send him the skin of an "o'api."

Johnston at once sent the prized bandoliers to England, where it was concluded they were zebra skin. A paper appeared announcing a new species of zebra from the Congo. Then Johnston received a package from Beni containing a skin and two skulls. The hoofs had dropped off the skin, but the bones clearly indicated there were two hoofs on each foot. Johnston noted the skull's bilobed lower canine teeth, which he knew to be characteristic of the giraffe, and realized the animal was a close relative.

Skin and skulls were sent to England. Excerpts of a letter and an exquisite water-color sketch of a pair of live okapis as imagined by the artist, Johnston, were displayed at the meeting of the Zoological Society of London on May 7, 1901. In the *Proceedings* of the next month there appeared a description of the okapi and the note that "Sir Harry Johnston, who was himself present, gave an account of the facts connected with his discovery of the Okapi." Sir E. Ray Lankester, later to write a monograph on the okapi, proposed its scientific name, *Okapia johnstoni.* The okapi was the last and only large mammal to elude scientists until the twentieth century.

Zoologists agreed that the okapi was a giraffid. They pondered what kind of giraffid. Was the okapi a degenerate giraffe, one that lost the long legs and long neck it once had, or did it, as Johnston himself first suggested, resemble the primitive fossil giraffid, *Palaeotragus?* They decided on the latter and grouped the okapi with the primitive giraffids, the palaeotragines. Its legs and neck never became elongate (as in the giraffine branch of the family tree), and its horns never underwent specialized development (as in the sivatheres). The okapi is, in fact, a "living fossil," an unspecialized descendant of the ancestral animal still living side by side with its highly specialized relative the giraffe.

In the okapi's survival through time habitat was probably the important factor. Okapis lived on in their deep, gloomy forests during the millions of years their sivathere and giraffine cousins, living out on the plains, were evolving their weird horn shapes, their long limbs and neck.

The okapi's world is one of gigantic water-laden trees, some towering 160 feet above the forest floor. Light filters through the constantly dripping treetop canopy. Flowering vines, palms, and ferns form the underbrush. Brown moldering leaves, soaked by frequent rains, cover the forest floor. Brightly colored birds flit through the trees. Black-and-white colobus monkeys leap from branch to branch or sit motionless, betrayed only by their long white tails. Bushbuck, bongo, duikers, giant forest hog, bushpig, the reddish dwarf forest buffalo, forest elephant, chimpanzee, leopard, and such smaller animals as pottos and pangolins share the okapi's forest home.

Through the gloom of the forest floor the shy okapi moves noiselessly. Its color and markings blend with the deep shadows. About the size of a large pony or a small horse, the okapi measures fifty-six to sixty inches at the shoulder and weighs between five and six hundred pounds. Female okapis tend to be larger than males. Like the giraffe, the okapi has a sloping back, but its strong, muscular neck is much shorter. Its legs are long, its head is delicately shaped, its large eyes are dark and limpid, its ears are enormous. Only the male okapi has horns, short, backward-projecting, and skin-covered except at their bony tips. The okapi's tail is shorter than the giraffe's and ends in a small tuft just above the hocks.

Okapi hair is velvety and varies from very dark brown

to dark chestnut with a purplish tinge to bright reddish bay. Beige to gray shades the sides of the head. Body color becomes almost black on the hindquarters, where bold black and white stripes form a pattern unique for each okapi. The forelegs are also conspicuously striped, black and white, and a stripe runs down from each "knee." The okapi's four fetlocks are broadly banded with black. Always well groomed in appearance, an okapi does much licking with its fourteen-inch-long, blue-gray tongue, which can reach even to its ear tips.

Active in daytime, the okapi moves within an area of about two square miles. It paces along well-trodden forest paths to visit certain places for feeding, resting, and depositing its dung. Because of its short, sturdy hoofs the okapi avoids marshy places and is careful where it crosses shallow streams. To drink, the okapi, like the giraffe, must splay its forelegs.

Okapis feed chiefly in early morning and late afternoon. Open forest glades where small streams produce lush vegetation are favorite browsing places. With its prehensile tongue the okapi grasps branches, strips off leaves, and pulls them into its mouth. For daytime standing the okapi prefers the base of a large tree. During a downpour it seeks shelter in thick undergrowth. At night the okapi selects a spot where there is little forest-floor vegetation to lie down.

Leopards and possibly snakes are the okapi's natural enemies, as well as the forest people who for centuries have hunted them. The okapi relies upon its keen sense of hearing. Its trumpetlike ears are forever moving to catch the slightest noises of the forest.

When frightened the okapi snorts and breaks into a gallop. With head and neck stretched out in front, it flees through the forest, jumping over fallen trees in its path. Although the stripe-patterned hindquarters may make it more difficult for a leopard to see the animal's outline, an okapi sometimes carries the raking scars of a leopard's claws. If an okapi is cornered it defends its life with powerful kicks and striking blows.

Except for now-and-then encounters, okapis usually lead solitary lives. Male okapis sometimes fight, swinging their heads to deliver blows on each other's rumps. At mating time the female okapi wanders through the forest plaintively trumpeting. Her calls and the scent trails left by front and hinds hoofs attract the male okapi. There is much ritual to okapi courtship. After repeated matings, male and female go their separate ways in the forest gloom. About fourteen months after mating, a gestation similar in duration to the giraffe's, the okapi drops her calf. Birth in the wild usually occurs from August to October, the time of heaviest rains.

The calf is marked like an adult okapi, but its color is very dark, almost black. A skimpy brownish-black mane extends down its neck and back onto its small rump. This mane persists as a ridge of very short stiff hairs on the neck of the adult.

It may take fifteen minutes of struggling attempts before the baby okapi is on its feet. Two and a half feet at the shoulder, it weighs about thirty-five pounds. Then, a half-hour old, the calf finds one of its mother's four teats and suckles hungrily. At six weeks the calf samples browse. Although cud-chewing commences at four months the calf continues to nurse until it is six to nine months old.

In the wild the baby okapi is hidden in the forest undergrowth. Probably this is why a zoo-born okapi calf spends much more time lying down than does its cousin the baby giraffe, born with the ability to keep up with a herd. At intervals the mother okapi comes to check on her calf. She cares for her baby much as a deer does its fawn. Even in zoos cow and calf okapis seldom stay in one part of their enclosure. If a keeper attempts to catch an okapi calf that runs after its mother, the baby's reaction often is to flop down, press its head to the ground, and flatten its ears against its neck. Presumably a leopard rushing at a cow and calf in the wild might not see the calf's instant reaction and would bound off through the forest vegetation in pursuit of the mother okapi. However, at least one okapi calf has been known to kick the zoo keeper.

Okapis are generally silent. Sometimes a cow "moos" to her calf. Calves have a bleating call. Zoo okapis, accustomed to one another's company, give low whistling calls when separated.

Because of their acute hearing, and to a lesser degree their sense of smell, okapis are almost impossible to come upon in the Ituri Forest. Even the Mbuti seldom see an okapi, but they do sometimes come upon a calf hidden in the underbrush. A Catholic missionary, Brother Joseph Hutsebaut, bottle-reared a succession of okapi calves brought to him by the Pygmies. Because of his way with okapis the Belgian government employed Brother Joseph for a time. In 1946 a government-controlled Okapi Capturing Station was established in the Ituri Forest, where the road north from Kisangani (Stanleyville) crosses the Epulu River.

Pits, dug on forest trails, are used to capture the okapis. The pits are six feet deep, smooth sided, and well floored with layers of leaves. Thin branches are crisscrossed over the pits and covered by rotted leaves and green foliage. If a duiker, a small forest antelope, tumbles into a pit it can spring out, but an okapi cannot.

When an okapi is captured, parallel stick fences are hastily constructed from pit to the nearest forest track or road. Here an earthen ramp is made, level with the back of a truck. On the back of the truck is a well-camouflaged stall. At the capture site the men dig away the front of the narrow pit. The okapi clambers up this ramp. Every effort is made not to frighten the animal. Slowly it paces its way along the fenced pathway and onto the truck. Once on the truck the narrow stall prevents the okapi from turning. The back of the truck is hastily closed.

As soon as the truck arrives at the Epulu Station the okapi is unloaded. Again it paces the length of a fenced corridor and into a forest enclosure. There are other okapis in paddocks nearby. With gentle handling an okapi quickly becomes tame. At Epulu it is possible to go in the paddocks and even pat the okapis. Okapis caught at Epulu have gone to leading zoos throughout the world. Some zoos have more than one okapi and are successfully breeding them in captivity.

Epulu is also a quarantine station where treatment is begun for parasitic worms that always infest okapis in the wild. Once rid of these parasites, an okapi has a better chance to survive in captivity. Okapis in zoos have lived as long as fifteen years.

The okapi's future in zoos seems secure. Its fate in the wild is less sure. Although ten thousand okapis are estimated to live in Zaïre, man's ever-increasing numbers will one day threaten the existence of the Ituri Forest. When this happens what will become of its shy inhabitant, the okapi?

15 The Future of Giraffes

Giraffes face an uncertain future. Africa, like the rest of the world, is undergoing a population explosion. Outside the national parks and reserves, encroaching human populations cause spreading patterns of cultivation. Habitat is destroyed as grasses are dug up and trees cut down and burned. Overgrazing by cattle, goats, and sheep, herded by the Masai and other pastoral tribes, denudes grazing lands. As suitable habitat dwindles, giraffes and other large mammals are driven off or destroyed. Within the parks, poaching, the illegal hunting of protected animals for meat and skins, is a serious threat. For how long and on what terms will giraffes and the other animals of Africa continue to share the modern world?

The future of giraffes depends upon the efforts of the African governments to conserve as part of their own natural heritage at least remnant animal populations within the parks and to increase man's understanding and appreciation of these ambling creatures, full of grace.

124

Glossary

Suggestions for Further Reading

Index

Glossary

abomasum: the last of the four chambers of the ruminant "stomach"

artiodactyls: animals, such as giraffes, that belong to the order of even-toed hoofed mammals, the Artiodactyla

browse line: the conspicuous effect of heavy giraffe browsing, which creates hour-glass shapes on larger trees and egg-shaped contours on bushes

browsing: feeding on leaves, buds, and twigs of trees and shrubs

bushveld: the belt of dry thornbush that stretches across Angola, South West Africa, Botswana, Rhodesia, and South Africa

estrus: a period in the female reproductive cycle when the animal is receptive to the male—that is, in heat

exostoses (singular, **exostosis**): bony bumps, such as those that develop on skulls of male giraffes

flehmen: the sampling of an interesting smell, especially of a female's urine by a male

head-slamming: the stylized fighting indulged in by bull giraffes which establishes the hierarchy of physical and sexual dominance

home range: the area over which an animal roams in feeding, mating, and rearing its young

leg beat: a bull giraffe, following closely a cow giraffe that is in heat, raises his foreleg and taps it against the cow's hindleg to test her readiness to be mounted

ligamentum nuchae: the neck ligament, enormously developed in the giraffe, for support of its head atop its columnar neck

miombo: the savanna of Africa's mid-continent, a vast area of grassland with scattered trees

nurseries: the "baby-sitting" or "auntie" arrangement in which one or two cows look after the giraffe calves in the herd; usually there are five or six calves in a nursery

nyika: the thornbush that covers the drier parts of eastern Kenya and Tanzania

omasum: the third of the four chambers of the ruminant "stomach"

ossicones: cartilaginous knobs; those on the skull of a new-born giraffe are precursors of the bony horns

rete: a network of blood vessels such as the giraffe's carotid rete, formed by division of the paired carotid arteries into hundreds of small twisting arteries; thought to have a cooling function in the giraffe

reticulum: the second of the four chambers of the ruminant "stomach"

rumen: the first of the four chambers of the ruminant "stomach" formed by a pouch in the wall of the esophagus

ruminants: herbivorous mammals that swallow their browsed or grazed food whole and later regurgitate it in cuds for thorough chewing; ruminants have four-part stomachs

tactile encounter: when a giraffe, or other animal, noses, licks, or rubs against another's body, neck, or head

water hole: any more or less permanent standing pool of water on desert, grassland, or savanna

Suggestions for Further Reading

Brown, Leslie. *Africa: A Natural History*. New York: Random House, 1965.

————. *The Life of the African Plains*. New York: McGraw-Hill Book Co., 1972.

Carr, Archie, and the editors of *Life*. *The Land and Wildlife of Africa*. New York: Time Inc., 1964.

Colbert, Edwin H. "The Giraffe and His Living Ancestor," *Natural History* 41 (1938), 46-50, 78.

Dagg, Anne Innis. "Giraffe Movement and the Neck," *Natural History* 72 (1962), 44-51.

Guggisberg, C. A. W. *Giraffes*. New York: Golden Press, 1969.

Laufer, Berthold. *The Giraffe in History and Art*. Chicago: Field Museum of Natural History, Anthropology Leaflet 27, 1928.

Leakey, Louis S. B. *The Wild Realm: Animals of East Africa*. Washington, D.C.: National Geographic Society, 1969.

Mochi, Ugo, and Carter, T. Donald. *Hoofed Mammals of the World*. New York: Charles Scribner's Sons, 1953; reissued 1971.

Spinage, Clive A. *Animals of East Africa*. Boston: Houghton Mifflin Co., 1963.

————. *The Book of the Giraffe*. Boston: Houghton Mifflin Co., 1968.

Van Citters, Robert L., Kemper, William S., and Franklin, Dean L. "Blood Pressure Responses of Wild Giraffes Studied by Radiotelemetry," *Science* 152 (1966), 384-86.

Index

131